STRANGE
BUT
TRUE?
CASEBOOK

Also available is the book of the first *Strange But True?* series:

Strange But True?: *Stories of the paranormal, from reincarnation and UFOs to poltergeists and psychic detectives*
(Piatkus Books, 1994)

JENNY RANDLES

STRANGE
BUT
TRUE?
CASEBOOK

INTRODUCED BY

MICHAEL ASPEL

PIATKUS

© 1995 LWT Productions Ltd
First published in 1995 by
Judy Piatkus (Publishers) Ltd
5 Windmill Street, London W1P 1HF

A catalogue record for this book
is available from the British Library

ISBN 0-7499-1558-7

Edited by Esther Jagger
Designed by Paul Saunders

Cover design by Jerry Goldie/Graphic Design
Photograph of Michael Aspel © LWT
Background photograph © Art Directors' Photo Library

Data capture and manipulation by
Create Publishing Services, Bath
Printed and bound in Great Britain by
The Bath Press Ltd, Bath, Avon

CONTENTS

PICTURE CREDITS

Permission to use copyright material is gratefully acknowledged to the following.

BLACK AND WHITE ILLUSTRATIONS: *pages 10-11* Simon Burt/*The Western Morning News;* *page 14* Scope Features; *page 19* *Oldham Evening Chronicle;* *page 26* Murray Sanders/*Daily Mail;* *page 35* Richard Weller-Poley Photography; *pages 38-39* Janet and Colin Bord/Fortean Picture Library; *page 43* PA News; *page 44* Mary Evans Picture Library; *page 45* Mary Evans Picture Library; *page 46* PA News; *page 49* PA News; *page 51* PA News; *page 52* Allan Lewis/Photo Press, Belfast; *page 53* *Sunday Life, Belfast;* *page 61* Adina Tovy/Robert Harding Picture Library; *page 63* Mary Evans Picture Library; *page 80* PA News; *page 83* John Paul Photography; *page 85* LWT; *page 87* Derek Ironside; *pages 90-91* Janet and Colin Bord/Fortean Picture Library; *page 95* Mike Wilson; *page 98* Simon Kench/Prospect Photographic Agency; *page 99* Bruce Smetham; *page 100* Simon Kench/Prospect Photographic Agency; *page 101* photograph by Mike Wilson and newspaper extract from the *Bridlington Free Press,* East Yorkshire; *pages 104, 106, 107, 111 and 113* The Pennington Family, Muncaster Castle; *pages 116 and 123* LWT; *pages 131, 132 and 134* reproduced by permission; *pages 140-141* Historic Scotland; *pages 148 and 149* Express Newspapers; *page 152* Brian Seward; *page 162* *The Dover Express;* *pages 164-165* Mary Evans Picture Library; *page 169* Mary Evans Picture Library; *page 173* Crown Copyright, reproduced with the permission of the Controller of Her Majesty's Stationery Office, reference PREMII/855 XC 21498; *page 174* LWT; *page 184* Channel 10 Australia. COLOUR ILLUSTRATIONS: *facing page 16* Scope Features; *facing page 17* Denes Natural Pet Care Ltd; *facing page 48* Martin McCullough/PA News; *facing page 112* The Pennington Family, Muncaster Castle; *facing page 113* The Pennington Family, Muncaster Castle; *facing page 144* Historic Scotland; *facing page 145* Brian Seward.

Whilst every effort has been made to trace all copyright holders, the publishers apologise to any holders not acknowledged.

ACKNOWLEDGEMENTS

LWT Productions would like to thank all those who have helped in the making of *Strange But True?*

If you've ever undergone an experience, or have other evidence or theories on the unexplained which we may be interested in for future programmes, please write to:

Strange But True?
LWT Productions
The London Television Centre
Upper Ground
London SE1 9LT

Programme Credits

RESEARCH
Daniel Barraclough, Rupert Smith, Mary Ramsay,
Roomana Mahmud, David Sayer

PRODUCER/DIRECTORS
Mike Brennan, Mike Adams, John Morgan, Steve Kelly,
Tracy Jeune, Mike Toppin, Humphrey Dixon, Nigel Miller

EXECUTIVE PRODUCER
Simon Shaps

EDITOR
Ralph Jones

FOREWORD

Welcome to another selection of extraordinary stories. As with our previous edition some of these accounts would be easy to dismiss if it weren't for the strength of the eyewitness testimony. I have to remind myself that inexplicable happenings can intrude into our lives in the most unexpected ways.

For instance, I think I came close to being an apparition myself once – and not just in the sense of being an image on a television screen.

Many years ago, when I was employed as a newsreader at the BBC, I'd arranged to meet some friends, who'd just moved into a flat near the studios, for a late night drink. It was possible, by leaving immediately after the bulletin, to be out of the building almost before the weather forecast began.

They'd left the door open, so in I went. Their television was still on. Tuned to BBC1. But the living room was deserted.

I could hear someone preparing a bath. It was about then, standing watching the TV and listening to the sound of running water, that I realized I was in the wrong flat. I made my excuses to a still empty room and left – quickly.

I like to think I didn't disturb their evening and that whoever it was didn't glance through their bathroom door and see me walking away from their television set, across their living room carpet and out of their flat, only a couple of minutes after seeing me live on the screen itself!

You will have to judge for yourself how many in this latest collection of stories from *Strange But True?* are bizarre coincidences and how many require some leap of faith.

Some of you may be happily reassured by the Lorraine Ham healing story, even though a physical explanation is hard to come by; others may take the great unsolved UFO sightings in their stride; or cheerfully accept the extraordinary eyewitness accounts of the phantom hitchhiker.

For myself, I like a good ghost story.

The most frightening ghost story I ever came across was a piece of fiction which intruded into the reality of my own life.

One summer's afternoon I wandered out into my garden and settled myself comfortably in the shade of a large tree. I'd just been given the collected ghost stories of M R James. There were over thirty of them. I picked one at random, *A School Story*. I began to read.

It began quietly enough. *The school was near London…* As I was.

A great white building with very fine grounds about it. Funny, there used to be a big old white house nearby.

There were large cedars in the gardens.

In the bright July sunlight the cedar above me shaded the pages I was reading.

It turned out that the author had set the story in Temple Fortune, East Sheen. My road was called Temple Sheen. I was sitting directly under the line of cedars mentioned in the opening pages. My garden was part of the old grounds of the big white house.

The date in the story was 24th July.

There was only the merest hesitation before I checked my watch. If the dates matched (as everything else had) it really wouldn't mean anything. It was a piece of fiction anyway.

I looked. It was 23rd July.

The story ended with two bodies locked in a deadly embrace at the bottom of a well. There, you will be relieved to know, the coincidences ended.

I hope you'll enjoy the stories that follow.

PART ONE

THE POWER OF HEALING

Undoubtedly one of the most dramatic areas of progress within paranormal research is that of psychic or spiritual healing. Not so long ago considered little better than witchcraft, it has rapidly developed into a legitimate practice winning over many sceptics within the medical profession.

Strange But True? has reported on that revolution by telling the story of one remarkable woman. But much has happened since we introduced her amazing talents in the first series.

Of course, if human beings can be healed by unseen forces, they may also be accused of using their own willpower. If they believe in the efficacy of a doctor – however odd that doctor's methods – then, perhaps, they may effect their own cure.

Yet, what if the same energies are unleashed upon creatures that cannot convince themselves they will get better? Can healing then still be all in the mind?

1

A NATURAL HEALER

Psychic healer Lorraine Ham featured in the first series of *Strange But True?* and in the accompanying book. Her appearance on the show provoked huge interest, and led to further dramatic evidence of her incredible abilities. As Lorraine explains: 'The response to the programme was enormous. The credits had not gone up at the end before the phone started to ring. It just rang continuously until about midnight – and by Monday letters were pouring in. By the end of the week the postman was actually bringing them in sacks. I had over six hundred on one day and it became quite overwhelming.'

Before the furore had begun to die down Lorraine had received twenty thousand calls for help. All of these had to be processed and she had to bring in other people to help with the work. The world of psychic healing faced a challenge the like of which it had never seen before. 'It is very difficult to pass letters on to someone else,' Lorraine points out. 'They were all desperate, and many were emotional pleas for help. Lots of them were from children and people with very serious illnesses, and all were deserving of some attention as soon as possible. But the sheer numbers prevented me from answering each one on its own. So I had a group of healers who came to help.'

A FATEFUL SLIP

Twelve-year-old Alison Drake loved to play soccer with the boys at school, but her pleasure was ruined one winter's day. She explains: 'I was walking down the garden path with a friend and it was really icy. I slipped on the step at the bottom and it was pretty painful. At the time I could get up and walk away – I just had quite a lot of pain in my back.' She was sent to bed by her mother, Christine,

Healer Lorraine Ham.

who hoped that the rest would put things right and that no serious damage had been done. But the pain simply got worse, and as Christine recalls: 'She was very tearful and distressed.'

Alison's parents decided to take her to their local doctor, who prescribed painkillers and sent her to a specialist at the Airedale Hospital. X-rays quickly revealed stress fractures at the base of Alison's spine. They might have been there since her birth, and had apparently become inflamed following her accident.

Dr John Cape, the consultant in charge, explains: 'Chronic lumbar pain in adolescents can be quite disabling. It can inhibit sporting activities and can also reduce the child's ability to take part in normal educational programmes because of inability to sit for protracted periods. When I met

PSYCHIC HEALING

Lorraine Ham works in West Yorkshire and is the great-great-granddaughter of a Maori herbalist and healer, a tribal chief from New Zealand. She appears to have inherited some of his skills, having practised healing with extraordinary success since 1970.

So remarkable have been her results that she became recognized by doctors working for the National Health Service in Yorkshire. Initially she applied her talents to cancer patients at the Cookridge Hospital in Leeds, where pain relief and counselling are vital to a patient's wellbeing. Lorraine showed a unique apti-

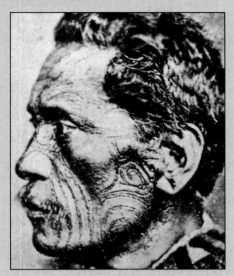

Chief Te Hau-Takiri Wharepapa, Lorraine's great-great-grandfather.

tude for this work. In 1990 she was invited by a GP at a local clinic to assist with his practice whenever her involvement seemed appropriate. Before long he was recommending patients to her on a regular basis and a highly unusual, but none the less successful, partnership has developed.

This foothold into the world of conventional medicine has been built upon by others, and Lorraine is not the only spiritual or psychic healer who works alongside professionally trained doctors. Those who have seen the benefits of such a relationship do not doubt that in the future this kind of complementary arrangement will be perceived as perfectly acceptable, even to the most old-fashioned of medical practitioners.

Lorraine Ham prefers not to call herself a psychic healer but to use the phrase 'natural healing' for the work that she does. Like most healers she has ideas but no certainty as to why it is successful; although most seem to follow similar methods, using their hands to transfer to the body of the patient what many think is a sort of energy.

Whether this is termed psychic, spiritual or natural healing, the only matter of any consequence is the relief that it can apparently bring to thousands of people. Explanations must take second place to the benefits.

Alison initially it was clear that she was quite demoralized by the on-going nature of the pain.'

Perhaps the main source of her distress was that taking part in football and other sports, such as ice-skating, now had to be placed on indefinite hold. As she was sent to see another specialist at the world-famous St James's Hospital in Leeds (colloquially known as 'Jimmy's'), her immediate prospects began to look bleak. Although the medical staff did all that could be done to ease her suffering, she was told that the best course of treatment was to watch and wait until, they hoped, the injury healed itself. Surgery was not considered a sensible option, given her age.

Christine Drake recalls the trauma of this period. 'Alison was only a teenager and yet she was living the life of an elderly lady. She could not walk properly and had to be helped up the stairs. Sometimes she just could not live life as a teenager at all. I was very upset, very frustrated. I wanted to help her and yet I couldn't. We had done everything we could with the medical profession, but they just were not getting any further.'

But then Christine saw the episode of *Strange But True?* that featured Lorraine Ham and decided, without telling her daughter, to join the thousands who would write and ask for help.

THE GENTLE TOUCH

Christine Drake's letter affected Lorraine Ham deeply, but when it arrived in October 1994 her calendar was fully booked. However, as the now teenage Alison lived close by she kept the letter on one side in case there was a cancellation. In February 1995 the opportunity arose.

Lorraine recalls that day. 'When Alison first came to see me she was in pain with her back and I did healing work there and then. I work differently with everybody, but it was appropriate to do it that way with her.' The session comprised a few minutes of relaxation therapy, during which Alison was so soothed that she almost drifted off to sleep. Then Lorraine began moving her hands lightly over the girl's body.

Alison remembers little of what followed, but she says: 'I felt relaxed, really relaxed and just at peace with myself, if you can understand that. I had my eyes closed, but I could feel warmth on the areas that she was healing and a sensation of all the pain drifting away. It was weird, but it felt brilliant that the pain was going.' She added that the sensation of heat was similar to 'a hot water bottle when it has been filled – that is, not hot, but not exactly lukewarm, just nice and pleasantly warm.'

Lorraine Ham demonstrating her healing technique on the Revd Alan Kitchen whom she successfully treated for neck problems in 1989.

Animal healer Charles Siddle believes that the spirit of the late famous vet Buster Lloyd Jones, pictured here, guides him in his work (see Chapter 2).

As Christine watched during these extraordinary few minutes she heard her daughter describe the odd sensations. 'The movement of Lorraine's hands seemed to be drawing the pain away from Alison, and this seemed to be following the direction of Lorraine's hands. I thought it was marvellous.'

From the healer's perspective, these events had a specific meaning. 'There was a shift of energies within her back and in her spine and the muscles around it. A lot of tension is alleviated and then the life force energies can flow more easily. So as I worked Alison was probably experiencing that shift in energy that allows for the bone to knit.'

Alison and her mother still have no idea what to expect long-term after the session, but were sure that it was worth giving healing a try. When they left the surgery the girl felt much better, but the pain later returned – at a lower level – and a second appointment with the healer was necessary. This relieved her suffering further and on what seems to be a much more permanent basis – so much so that a third session was cancelled when Christine Drake phoned Lorraine and asked if it was needed. Alison was doing PE at school for the first time in almost four years and was otherwise fit and well.

As Alison now reports: 'I feel like I have my life back.' She can now do all the things she has longed for since that terrible day in 1991. Lorraine Ham will monitor progress and be on call should her services be required again. Everyone hopes, of course, that they will not.

THE ROAD TO WEMBLEY

For Alison Drake her love of football was just part of teenage life, but for Craig Flemming it was his livelihood. If he was no longer able to kick a ball around the pitch his whole future could be in jeopardy. This was the situation that confronted Lorraine Ham when she read yet another of the countless letters flooding in to her box number; this one prominently displayed the logo of Oldham Athletic Football Club .

Craig was a star young midfield player for this First Division soccer team who had battled their way to an FA Cup semi-final with Manchester United at Wembley in April 1994. Sports writers raved about his performance in keeping multi-million-pound international Mark Hughes at bay. The Premier League sides were watching him eagerly and he was widely tipped for great things. Then the greatest fear of all footballers struck out of nowhere – the kind of intractable injury that can potentially destroy their career. Craig describes the pain that he was feeling. At first there was 'just tightness as the game went on. This progressed into the hip and front of the thigh and the pain got worse as I played on.'

In the summer break after the 1993-4 season the rest helped Craig considerably. He was on anti-inflammatory tablets to try to ease the situation, but by the third match of the following season the pain had struck again. It was now a struggle for him to complete a match and he began to worry about his future, despite medical opinion that there was nothing seriously wrong with him and that it was certainly not an injury that would end his playing days. But as the pain refused to go away his fears quite naturally developed. Then, after a particularly traumatic time on the pitch against Southend, he knew that action had to be taken. 'The pain was that bad there was no other choice,' he explains.

His wife, Nicola, confirms: 'We realized that he could not keep going any more.' It affected him badly: 'All he wanted to do was play football. He was just so fed up because he couldn't do anything about it and there wasn't somebody saying, "You have broken your leg and you'll be back in however many weeks or months it takes." Of course, when a footballer cannot play, the danger is that some rising youngster will snatch his place in the team on a permanent basis.'

For Craig the misery ran deeper because he had a whole series of niggling problems. His club sent him for surgery to repair a torn abdominal muscle that had been diagnosed. This helped to alleviate the pain, but did not completely solve the problem.

He says: 'I was still left with this pain in the groin and the hip. After about eight weeks – when I should have been back playing after that kind of operation – I wasn't. They tried building my groin with weights. But that wasn't working.' Injury problems that should have been resolving themselves were forcing him out of the game he loved.

MAKING OLDHAM MORE ATHLETIC

Dennis Wright was the physiotherapist at Oldham who was struggling to bring his star player back to fitness. When it was apparent that the injury was not clearing up as fast as was hoped, there was concern. 'This was a tremendous blow to the club because they had anticipated that after this initial surgery he would be back into the fray again. All the recognized physiotherapeutic procedures were tried, with the expected slight improvement, but we just could not tip the balance in favour of saying, "Well, next week he'll be fit to play."'

A second operation followed, this one designed to release the tendon in his leg. Craig recalls: 'That released a lot of the pressure in there but there was still

Craig Flemming playing for Oldham Athletic against Southampton in May 1993.

a pain. I was getting a lot more movement, but it was still sore when I actually did things.'

In November Nicola heard about Lorraine Ham via *Strange But True?* and decided to write for help. Craig says that this was when he was at his lowest ebb, in the weeks between the two operations: 'I didn't seem to be getting anywhere, so I thought I would give it a go. I didn't have anything to lose. I mean, if it didn't work, it didn't work. But I was convinced that it would do.'

It was to be March 1995 before the session with Lorraine could be arranged. Then he and Nicola went to visit her and were pleasantly surprised by the friendly, calming atmosphere. Craig says of the treatment: 'You do feel totally at ease with yourself.' As the healer moved her hands around his body there was an odd sensation. 'It was a bit like pins and needles, or if you put your hands next to a TV set and you get the static – that kind of feeling moving around my body.' When the session was over there was no further trace of this feeling. It only occurred when Lorraine Ham was holding her hands close to his body.

Arriving at the Oldham ground, Boundary Park, for training the following Monday, Craig was wary of what to expect. He worked out with Dennis Wright and tried the exercises that had been giving him pain before. 'I let my leg go all the way down and brought it back up again and there was no pain at all. So then I just went on doing these exercises all day. I was a bit flabbergasted by it.'

Dennis Wright says he is 'the last person in the world to be involved in fringe medicine'. But he saw how dramatically painfree Craig now appeared to be. 'It was disappointing from my point of view. I asked myself: had I failed and yet somebody else succeeded? In trying to rationalize, and one does try, I wondered had somebody produced a relaxation that we had failed to do? The answer must be yes, because he claimed he was painfree and had quite a wide range of movement.'

Craig believes that the medical treatment he received was a great help to his recovery. He simply needed an extra push – possibly to get over a mental as well as a physical barrier. Lorraine Ham provided that. 'I really don't know how it worked,' he adds. 'I just know it did.'

As Craig prepares to fight for his first team place in the 1995-6 season, Dennis Wright concurs that his progress has been immense. 'It's quite exhilarating. Who cares what produces the result?'

ALL IN THE MIND?

There are those who would argue that Lorraine Ham is able to achieve such success because her patients believe in her ability. Indeed, many of them clearly do – but does this allow them to overcome the mental barriers that can be erected by the subconscious mind on the road to physical wellbeing? This viewpoint is, of course, the origin of the term 'faith healing', used in a derogatory sense to diminish any truly mysterious powers that might be at work. Whilst it is conceivable that a case such as Craig Flemming's could owe something to his own will to get better, is this always the case? Lorraine Ham certainly does not believe so.

'I think that the body does have the power to heal itself,' she says. 'Healing energies – whether they are in the form of an energy provided by, or channelled through, a healer, or energy that comes through medicine – these are just ways to help that person's own powers to heal themselves.' Furthermore, 'a person who is positive about his healing can improve more quickly than someone who is not, but healing can still work with someone who is quite sceptical'.

She is adamant that willpower alone is not enough to be effective. There has to be something more that is taking place. However, perhaps one of the strongest arguments in favour of the influence of self-belief is the efficiency of absent healing. If the healer is not present to transfer any energy, then how can this be the cause of any progress?

ABSENT HEALING

As its name suggests, absent healing occurs when there is no direct link between the healer and their patient. They may be separated by hundreds, even thousands, of miles. But an attempt will be made to send 'healing vibrations' to bring about an improvement.

Since Lorraine's TV appearance a National Healing Centre which uses absent healing has been set up. Based in Shrewsbury, it links up a whole network of healers from around the UK who meditate three times a day on the many people whom Lorraine Ham cannot see as a patient in a normal clinical environment. This has been invaluable, for if Lorraine had to meet face to face with every one of the twenty thousand people who had written to her, then twenty-four hours a day and seven days a week would not be long enough.

She explains: 'It was obvious from the number of people who were writing that there was a very definite need for some form of help. I could not write to everybody or see them for private healing sessions. So I decided to put them on to an absent healing list.' These people were all advised of what was happening and the length of time for which this mass exercise in healing powers would be in operation.

Ruth Dorrington was one of those contacted by Lorraine and told that she would be in receipt of absent healing for six weeks, at 6.30 a.m., 12.30 p.m. and 10.30 p.m. each day. Ruth was a serious athlete – a club runner preparing for the 1995 road racing season. But then she was struck down by a hip injury. The tendons were badly affected and, despite help from her physiotherapist, she had to curtail her training regime considerably. This greatly reduced her chances for the coming races. Then she saw Lorraine Ham on *Strange But True?* and was immediately filled with hope. 'I was very optimistic that this was the route to immediate recovery,' she explains.

However, Lorraine replied it was not possible to fit in a visit to her surgery in Yorkshire. Ruth explains: 'When I got the letter back I didn't really know what absent healing was. I didn't really try to find out, either, but I thought it might help. And I did start to feel better. I was not entirely sure why, but it seemed too coincidental that I had started to feel better at that period of time.'

When the absent healing session from the centre was concluded, Ruth was almost fully recovered. 'The end of the six-week period coincided with the time when I felt I was fit enough to get back on to a proper training schedule and race seriously. I wasn't sure if it was coincidence, or whether it was natural progression, but I felt the healing had definitely been a contributory factor.' But was this recovery the result of a psychosomatic process – her faith in the capacity for healing to work having simply speeded up her body's natural regeneration?

Ruth doubts that. 'It was not some sort of psychosomatic thing where I thought – oh, good, there are lots of people thinking about me. I really did not think about it that much.' She just notes that after weeks of getting nowhere, 'sort of one step forward, two steps back', when the absent healing was in force 'suddenly progress was all in the right direction'. Now she presumes that, with so many healers having focused their thoughts at once, 'then all that energy has got to be good. It has got to heal me. And it seemed to do the trick.'

Lorraine Ham is very hopeful that the new National Healing Centre will fulfil the needs of many sick people. Already its absent healing lists are swelling as those who believe they have been helped by the unusual method tell their friends and relatives. Potentially, this form of healing seems to have an unlimited future. Lorraine is also sure that the Centre's success is not entirely due to mind over matter. 'In some cases it may be psychosomatic, but not in every case. There are people that have very definite physical ailments that have improved through receiving absent

```
                    LORRAINE RIKA-HAM
                 NATIONAL HEALING CENTRE
                    ROLAND THOMAS HOUSE
             ROYAL SHREWSBURY HOSPITAL SOUTH
                 SHREWSBURY   SY3 8XF
```

Dear Ruth

Thank you for your letter. The response to recent publicity
has been quite remarkable and I apologise for having taken so
long to reply. I would dearly love to have been able to meet
and work with everyone who has taken the trouble to write but
on a one to one basis that is not possible.

Everyone who writes is put on the absent healing list. No
details are given and strict codes of confidentiality are
observed. However, it may comfort you to know that a network
of loving, caring people covering areas throughout the country
are sending you their healing love at least three times a day.
Your name will be deleted from the list 12 weeks from the date
of this letter unless you advise otherwise.

I am also sending you the name and address of a healer in your
region. The healers I refer are not necessarily known to me
personally but have been put forward by the healing

          are avail   Please   rk the   ide
your envelope WORKSHOP.

My thoughts and those of my colleagues and friends who work
together send you love and blessings for your healing.

With Love, Light and Peace

Extracts from the letter Ruth received informing her that she was on Lorraine's absent healing list.

healing. We could say that maybe they would have improved anyway and it was the right time for them to get better. But at the end of the day it doesn't really matter so long as they get the desired result.' Ruth Dorrington would certainly agree. She is now running better than ever and has broken several club records since her absent healing session. She knows that Lorraine Ham had a hand in that achievement – but she does not have a clue how it worked!

2

ALL GOD'S CREATURES

I f it is possible to heal human beings through spiritual energy, what of God's other creatures? Can they too be freed from their pain and suffering by the mysteries of psychic healing? Certainly you would get a positive response from the many patients who visit clinics held by Nicky Prouvost in the pretty market town of Totnes in rural Devon.

Nicky, a thin-faced, amiable Frenchwoman, sees everything from rats to Pekinese, and applies the most remarkable methods to nurse them back to vitality. The reaction of their delighted owners says it all. 'Since we brought Pickles to Nicky for healing he is a lot happier. He is a lot more comfortable and has more energy ... I am convinced it is the healing. I think the healing is wonderful,' beams one owner who has seen a painful skin irritation disappear from her pet. 'Poppy had a phantom pregnancy,' another explains about her dog. 'The physical symptoms were quite distressing .... We brought her to Nicky and this improved her mental state and her physical health to the state which you see now – a happy dog with a shiny coat.'

A third owner has made several visits to this special surgery with her dog Trish, after the vet had told her that Trish would lose the use of both hind legs. Smiling at the healthy-looking animal frolicking before her, Trish's owner reports: 'I've seen a remarkable improvement. She seems much better and that's all I need to know .... Now she is walking and running around happily.' Another added about her dog's condition: 'It's incurable, so anything that can relieve the pain must be a good thing.'

HEALING HANDS

But how on earth does Nicky Prouvost – an ordinary woman without any training as a conventional vet – manage to bring about such dramatic transformations? 'I don't know what it is that I am doing,' Nicky cautiously reports. 'I cannot explain how it works. I just put my hands on the animal and let them go where they want upon the body. I am not guiding them myself. I am channelling a healing energy which comes from somewhere else. I don't know where.'

Concentrating intensely as she works, she moves her hands across the strange assortment of creatures brought to her Pets' Healing Clinic. There are rabbits, hamsters, ducks and even sheep, as well as countless dogs, who look faintly perplexed as the healer traverses their widely varying body shapes. They certainly appear to show no hint of distress as the session unfolds.

Nicky always ensures that an owner has been to see a vet before they come to her clinic. However, 'When an owner tells me about the diagnosis of a vet, I cannot say that it really makes a difference for me, because whatever needs to be healed in an animal will be healed.' As she points out, sometimes the cause of an illness may be hidden from conventional medicine. But she believes that the energy channelled through her hands reaches the source to correct whatever problem is to blame.

How did this remarkable ability begin? Surprisingly, as a child Nicky was not unduly sentimental about animals – her family had just a working dog, used for hunting and never really viewed as a pet. It was only after she moved to Devon and her cat became ill that Nicky discovered she could help relieve its suffering by way of some unknown power.

Once the news of her secret was out, Nicky's friends flocked to her with their own pets and she was set on her way towards a healing career. But she is adamant that there is nothing special about her skills. 'I do not believe there are gifted people who have the power of healing. I think this is an energy that we can all tap into. We all somewhere have this ability. We might have lost contact with it. We might not be aware of it. But I strongly believe that healing is an integral part of us all.'

As for the future, she is very optimistic. 'I am very excited, because I feel that there is definitely a growing interest in the healing of animals. People are becoming more inquisitive about the different ways of treatment and

Opposite *Nicky Prouvost with one of her patients.*

Daily Mail, Thursday, May 18, 1995

The woman who heals animals vets can't help

Headline from the Daily Mail, *May 18, 1995.*

healing is becoming more acceptable. They are also more willing to try it out.'

As a result many animals, who cannot express their gratitude in any obvious way, may have a great deal to thank Nicky and her healing crusade for.

VETTING THE EVIDENCE

Although healers such as Nicky would argue that the results are measured in the joy expressed by her patients' owners, more traditional vets are not so sure. Nicholas Munnings has some support to offer. He runs his practice in Devon along conventional lines, but does allow for a number of alternative methods to be used. 'In my practice over the last ten years I have been using homeopathy and recently acupuncture and have been delighted with the results in certain cases. This is something borne out through the human population on a regular basis.'

However, he insists that these methods have a logical grounding. Certainly some semblance of rational science can be put forward in an attempt to suggest how they might work. But with what he terms 'faith healing' that is more difficult. 'Unfortunately, there does not seem to be a scientific basis for that.' Nor, he adds, has he got any successful results. 'When we have been back through the cases where I am aware that healing has been used on chronically ill animals then I have not seen any of them suddenly make a miraculous recovery. It would be very unwise, I feel, for anybody to take an acutely ill animal for faith healing. However, I think I have got to say that it cannot be harmful to the animals, unless an obvious illness is not treated quickly enough because people go to a healer first. I would desperately love it to be of benefit, because I think the more alternative therapies that we have to help out animals must be good. No single therapy has the answer.'

Even more outspoken is Paul DeVile, President of the British Veterinary Association, whose members undergo five years of training, none of which takes spiritual healing into account.

'We are scientists and our training is based on science. Therefore, as a profession, and certainly as an association, we could not accept any forms of treatment that are not based on science. I have no knowledge of any case in my particular practice where spiritual healing has caused an improvement in the animal. I do not say it has caused any deterioration, but I know of no case that has succeeded.'

He points out that, when the veterinary homeopathists applied for affiliation to the national association, this was rejected by its council. Moreover, 'Any person who practises veterinary medicine – that is to say makes a diagnosis and treats an animal without reference to a veterinary surgeon – is actually breaking the law via the Veterinary Surgeons Act of 1966.' However, he does recognise that it sometimes 'might be in the better interest of the client and the animal to let them take their pet to undergo some form of alternative medicine like healing'.

CRYSTAL CLEAR

Not all vets are quite so distrustful of spiritual healers. Richard Allport runs a practice in Potters Bar, Hertfordshire. He qualified as a veterinary surgeon in 1973, and for many years applied only conventional methods. But he found that some animals were suffering from the side-effects of the drugs that he administered. Also, a few illnesses were being controlled, but not cured, and so the animals had to return for regular attention. It was at this

NATURAL MEDICINE

For centuries, mankind has practised various types of natural healing. These include acupuncture, an ancient method of treatment developed by the Chinese. Today it is one of the most common forms of alternative therapy used on humans and also on animals. Long needles are gently inserted into the skin of the patient, at carefully selected 'pressure points'. Each of these is said to reflect a node of some internal energy system which keeps the body in balance.

Modern science suspects that acupuncture may work by way of the electrical fields which course through the human body and thus help to maintain proper order in this.

There is an interesting parallel between this use of needles placed into a network of energy paths (known as meridians) across the body and needle like stones (or megaliths) erected by ancient cultures at selected locations in the earth's surface. These may have been designed to perform a similar function on the recently discovered electromagnetic biosphere of our planet.

Homeopathy is another increasingly popular form of alternative therapy. In some ways it is a sophisticated folk medicine and uses commonly occurring substances in its treatment programme, either applied as poultices or taken orally. The concept is to regard the living person holistically (ie as a whole entity) and in respect to their perceived needs using 'like for like' methods rather than in response to the symptoms of a particular illness.

Some of the natural medicines used may be poisonous or even deadly when taken in more than the minute amounts prescribed. However, whilst some of these practices were based on folklore or magical beliefs, many were developed by trial and error across the centuries. What was found to work became a secret passed down through countless generations of healers.

The skill of the homeopath therefore is gained from old practices but its knowledge can be applied in the modern world to treat conditions that science may as yet be incapable of dealing with. Natural remedies are also regarded by many as being better than costly artificial drugs because they do not induce the ugly side effects that some medicines can bring.

point that he decided to look for other possibilities.

'My wife was an occupational health nurse and one of the men at her place of work was a very good healer. He helped her with a back problem, and she was convinced,' he said. Soon afterwards Richard was recommended to a man called Charles Siddle who was doing healing work on animals. Now Charles has a weekly clinic at Richard's practice; his patients are often passed on to him by Richard or other vets.

Richard Allport comments: 'I know what he's doing, but I don't know how he does it. There is no doubt that he has healed and helped to heal many of my patients and patients referred from other practices. My own feeling is that healing is some sort of energy transfer and Charles is some sort of conductor. But what the energy consists of and whether one could measure it, I don't know. All I know is that it works. It's safe and dogs and cats are helped by it. I am not saying that it is going to be a cure-all, but I think it can help.'

Animal healer Charles Siddle.

The method that Charles Siddle uses may seem a little curious at first. In addition to the laying on of hands he travels with a large white crystal which he places beside the animal to be treated. Not only that, but he believes he is guided by the spirit of a famous vet who died in 1980.

The white beard and care-worn features reflect his gentle manner as Charles Siddle describes what occurred. 'I used to meet Buster Lloyd Jones at dog shows such as Crufts. He told me that I could heal, but I did not believe him. When he passed over I got involved in seeing a horse. One day in the stable Buster appeared in his physical form and said that he had come back because he wanted me to do healing and that he would work through me.'

Charles explains that he contacts the deceased vet whenever a new case comes along, and Buster's spirit form makes a visit ahead of him to assess the problem. By the time his earthly counterpart reaches the sick animal, his mentor from the spirit world is able to convey the diagnosis and begin the healing. Charles Siddle is therefore merely the conduit. All the work is done from the vet on the other side.

Left *Charles Siddle while a pupil at Harrow Boys' School (centre).*

Below *During his days as a pet shop owner.*

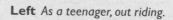

Left *As a teenager, out riding.*

An Early Success

One of Charles Siddle's early successes was with Orion Blaze (pictured over-leaf), a talented showjumper valued at £40,000. Owner Trina Lewis had great hopes for him until a disastrous day when he tripped whilst out walking and tore the muscles in one of his forelegs.

'The vet came to see him and said he should have nine months' stable rest,' said Trina. This advice was followed and, with regular check-ups, he was finally given the all clear. But, 'On the second day Orion escaped from his stable and went absolutely berserk. He ran down the driveway and turned into a maniac. When I eventually caught him his leg had come up. His injury had re-occurred.'

The disappointed vet announced that further lengthy rest was the best course of treatment. However, Trina, now desperate, had heard of Charles Siddle's reputation and decided to give it a try. However, when the healer arrived at the stable she felt far from enthusiastic. He placed his crystal in the hay, then, as Trina remembers: 'put his hands on the horse's leg and put some hose water on the leg as well. Having done that he said that the horse would be fine and asked me for £25.' She added, laughing: 'I thought I'd been robbed!'

But the next day Orion Blaze's condition showed a remarkable improve-ment. The swelling had gone down and so Trina took him out for a gentle walk. From that point he progressed so rapidly that he was soon entering and winning competitions in a higher class than before. As Trina comments, mustering all her objectivity, 'There must be something to healing. I am still very sceptical about this sort of thing, but obviously with this case it seems to have helped. I am prepared to keep an open mind.'

Jessica's Case

In a case such as that of Orion Blaze there must always be room for doubt. Perhaps he would have improved anyway, because of the stable rest. Healing seems to have been a factor, but can never be proven. However, when it comes to Jessica's condition there seems no alternative to a miracle.

She was one of many horses in Jan Piper's stables, and in 1992 it was antici-pated that this gentle mare would have more foals to follow the two race winners to which she had already given birth. Then Jan noticed something wrong with the animal, who had been off her food for a short while. 'A small lump appeared on her left eyelid. But it didn't worry me too much at first.' She thought it was just a cyst, but when it started to grow she became more concerned and called in her vet, Mark Sinnott.

Mark knew the horses well, having dealt with the stables for many years. He noted that Jessica was rather thin, and took blood and fluid samples for further investigation. Eventually he arranged for the animal to visit the Animal Health Trust in Newmarket where the lumps were removed under anaesthetic and sent to a pathologist for a detailed biopsy.

Mark explained: 'The pathology tests showed that Jessica's condition was equine lymphosarcoma, which is a type of white cell cancer. It is quite rare and usually spreads to other parts of the body internally.' There were other lumps on the horse's groin and further blood tests indicated that the disease was spreading. It was bad news that he had to break to his client, but Jan Piper took it philosophically. As an owner of many horses it was the sort of thing that she has had to learn to live with. But the news was still a blow, because the mare was her favourite and loved by all the stable hands.

'This condition has an extremely poor prognosis,' Mark continued. Horses usually deteriorate quite rapidly, and there is no known cure for this form of cancer. Chemotherapy may be a potential treatment in the future, but at the moment once the diagnosis is made the horse usually ends up having to be put to sleep.'

ONE LAST HOPE

The idea of letting Jessica be seen by a healer was regarded as absurd when it first came up in Jan's conversation with a friend. But, as she says: 'You start to clutch at straws and you have nothing to lose. So I tried to convince my husband Graham, who at first said it was a load of poppycock and that I was just giving myself false hope.' Eventually, however, Jan made Graham realize that Jessica was going to die anyway if nothing was done, and that Charles Siddle was worth a try. Reluctantly, he agreed.

'When Charles Siddle arrived I was not quite sure what to expect,' Jan says. 'I did not know if he would wear funny clothes. I must admit I kept laughing about it, but when he came he was quite normal. That was a shock. He walked up to Jessica and he was very polite. He went into the stable and spoke to her a lot. He laid his hands on her and he was talking all the time. He didn't seem to take very long but was just running his hands all over her body and the particular places where the lumps were. Then he just stepped back and said "That's it – she'll be fine now". I mean, he was so confident!'

As the healer describes it: 'When I got there I rather thought that the

One of Siddle's early successes, Orion Blaze, ridden here by Trina Lewis.

family did not believe what I could do. But after talking to Buster and looking at the horse I was quite convinced that we could do something for her. I
gave her the healing and told them to put rugs on her and not take them off
until Monday morning.'

He explains that the incessant talking, usually assumed by a client to be
between himself and the animal, is really his conversation in a trance-like
state with the spirit of the late Buster Lloyd Jones, who is in charge of everything that happens. 'I cannot remember at all how long I was in the stable.
But when I left I knew Jessica would be all right because Buster told me that
she would be.'

When Graham Piper returned later that day he was completely unconvinced that anything had happened. The horse looked no different and was
still, as far as he could tell, in terminal decline. But the very next morning
something amazing happened. Stable hand Mandy Drummond describes

what took place. 'I got to her stall and Jessy had eaten all her hay. She looked over the door at me and her eyes were bright. Her ears were pricked up and she was calling and kicking at the door for food.'

Mandy called Jan over and they both stared in astonishment at the horse. As Mandy added: 'I wanted to believe that Charles could cure her. But I didn't actually think he could do anything. It was a very strange situation – a little man coming and putting his hands on a horse, trying to cure her of cancer. I never thought it would work.'

But work it did, for Jessica's health returned to normal and many of the lumps faded within a couple of weeks. Three years later she is still fighting fit and has had another foal which looks like becoming a winner on the track.

'Jessica has simply never looked back and as a result,' Jan Piper asserts, 'My attitude towards healing has completely changed. I did not believe one little bit in it. It would never have entered my head to use a healer. Now I wouldn't hesitate. If anything happened to any of the horses I'd phone Charles straightaway. It's a miracle. Really, I cannot explain why she is still alive.'

It's a Miracle

Often, when human beings are healed, it is argued that they mobilize their own natural bodily defences by believing so strongly in the powers of the healer. A psychosomatic (or mind over matter) type of cure is then effected. The same principle operates when a patient is given a tablet which has no real reason to work – but he or she believes that it can. Such a drug is called a placebo and is often prescribed to speed recovery where the patient's mental state is considered to be important.

But how can this work with animals? Vet Richard Allport remarks: 'I would say that animals do not experience a placebo effect. They cannot imagine that they are going to get better. So if the animals respond – and in my experience they do – then it must be a real healing effect.'

Richard was speaking generally and not of Jessica's specific case. What is the medical opinion of this alleged miracle? Her vet, Mark Sinnott, returned to see Jessica a few weeks after her amazing recovery. He was very surprised by her healthy condition and made various enquiries about what could have happened. 'I discussed her case with other vets and they are of the opinion that no horse has ever recovered from equine lymphosarcoma. By all the laws of veterinary medicine Jessica should be dead by now, but she's still walking around happily in the field with a foal. This is something that we cannot explain.'

Jessica, after her miraculous recovery, with her foal, Frank, in April 1994.

How such healing works remains a mystery. Yet, from cases such as Jessica's – despite reluctance to believe on the part of animal owners and veterinary authorities alike – it seems that somehow it can effect the most remarkable cure. To the person who sees their pet rescued from debilitating illness, or even from death, continued wellbeing is all the proof that they will ever need.

QUE SOY
ERA
IMMACULADA COUNCEPCIOU!

PART TWO

THE AGE OF MIRACLES

It's a miracle! This phrase is widely used in today's world – yet how often do we mean it?

In an age of technology and science a miracle seems oddly out of place. Surely these days nothing is so impossible that it must be considered a product of divine intervention?

Yet, according to the testimony of ordinary folk caught up in them, there are miracles taking place. They have even spawned their own bureaucracy – a committee regularly meets in the Vatican to pass judgement on their merits.

Strange But True? reports not only on some real life modern miracles which defy logic and understanding but also follows the traditional and hallowed process by which miracles are examined and evaluated.

3

THE POWER OF PRAYER

Marion Carroll was a young Irishwoman full of the joys of life who loved to go out dancing with her husband, Jimmy. In 1972 she had just had her first child, Anthony. Then, out of nowhere, tragedy struck.

'I was always wearing high heels, because I was so small,' she says, trying to understand the pains that beset her. 'When I became pregnant with Anthony in December I was very ill, but I thought it was just the pregnancy. But after Anthony was born I lost the power in my right leg.' The problems continued to mount as Marion struggled to bring up her young son. Jimmy was in the army and away a good deal, which made things even more difficult.

'Anthony was only a few months old when my leg started giving trouble,' Marion explains. 'I woke up one morning – we'd been out the night before to my parents' wedding anniversary – and my leg felt numb and there was pain in it. I thought it was just the dancing the night before.'

When she realized that the pain was not going away she went to her doctor, who suggested that it was probably just flu causing her to suffer a few aches and pains. But as time passed and she felt no better the possibility of a slipped disc was discussed, and Marion went to hospital for an investigation. A few days later she left for home on crutches, worse than ever – and the doctors were no nearer to finding a solution to an illness that was rapidly crippling this once lively and active young mother.

Before long Marion was sent to see a psychiatrist, to explore the option that the pains might be caused by some nervous disorder. However, this possibility was soon rejected by the psychiatrist, who insisted, 'If all my patients came in like you I'd be out of a job!'

In 1976 she experienced her second traumatic pregnancy, when her daughter Cora was born by Caesarian section. Marion spent much of the preceding nine months in hospital and emerged from this experience with further problems: blackouts, eye trouble, continued debilitation in her limbs and the onset of kidney infections. It was clear that something was seriously wrong. She was sent from hospital to hospital as the doctors tried desperately to discover what was causing her symptoms. But after giving her every imaginable kind of scan, they were no closer to being able to offer any positive help.

'I got a lot worse with the kidney infections,' she says, 'and I was rushed in one Tuesday. I don't remember much of what happened after that. I know I felt funny on my right side, that's all.'

In fact, the doctors were planning exploratory surgery when she saw a neurologist in Dublin. According to Jim Carroll, the doctor questioned her carefully and then sent for him. He says that the specialist reported that Marion could have MS – multiple sclerosis. There was no cure.

THE DEPTHS OF DESPAIR

Marion's initial reaction might seem strange. 'I was thrilled, because at long last they had discovered what was wrong with me. I knew what multiple sclerosis was and I didn't care. It was not until I got home from Dublin, when I had the nurse and home help every day and my neighbours and friends were coming in to see me and they were looking very sorrowful – some were actually crying – that I remember thinking to myself: I have only a few weeks to live.'

Of course, she was wrong. MS sufferers do tend to deteriorate over time but can survive for years with proper care. However, during the 1980s Marion discovered just what the fateful diagnosis meant to her life as she became so ill that she could hardly do anything for herself. 'I ended up in a wheelchair. Then my kidneys and bladder started giving me trouble and I had a catheter inserted. A while after that I lost the complete power of my right arm and hand and only had limited power in my left. I was completely blind in my right eye and had very little sight in my left eye. My speech had become badly affected, the muscles of my throat being constricted. Eventually I had to wear a collar to support my neck and head.'

Jimmy describes the strain of coping with his job, caring for young children and being a nurse to his disabled wife. 'I'd get up in the morning at seven o'clock, get the kids ready for school. I had a special chair in which Marion had to be washed every day. I used to put her into the chair, bring her down to the bathroom and shower her and put her back into bed again.

Everything had to be done for her. Every time she had to be moved, I had to move her. I remember one day I came home from work to find Marion in the middle of the floor. She was stuck. She had an electric wheelchair with left–hand controls. Her right foot had fallen down off the stand and was caught under the wheel. She'd been there for two hours.' Before long Marion had to be tied into the wheelchair as her balance had gone completely.

And so it went on, day after day, year after year, without hope of improvement and only a gradual decline facing the two of them. There seemed no way out. The doctors were doing all that they could, but this was little more than pain control to provide a few brief periods of remission during which Marion's condition improved for a short while. But afterwards it always got worse again. Eventually, they knew, some complication would arise which would result in her death. Despite their fervent religious convictions and the saying of prayers and the rosary, Marion and Jimmy Carroll were expecting no miracles. They were just grateful for every extra day that God gave them.

A PLACE OF FAITH

The road sign at the outskirts of Knock, in Gaelic and English.

Knock is perhaps the most famous shrine of the Irish Catholic Church. More than a century ago a group of villagers in this hamlet claimed to have seen a vision of the Virgin Mary outside the church. This now houses a sculpture replica of the vision. A new basilica has since been built on the site and the shrine now draws a million visitors every year. Many of them are sick and go in hope of finding a miraculous cure.

Marion had already made the journey from her home in Athlone, County Westmeath twice before when her health had been better, but without any result. Now, particularly since her condition had declined so much and travelling would be uncomfortable, she was unwilling to join members of her local diocese who were about to make another pilgrimage to the shrine. She only said yes when Gerry Glynn, who would be driving the ambulance for the Order of Malta Corps, asked her to go because she did not have the heart to say no to his kindness.

VISIONS OF THE VIRGIN

The vision of the Virgin Mary at Knock ranks alongside the apparitions at Lourdes in France and Fatima in Portugal. On the night of 21 August 1879 fifteen witnesses saw an altar with a lamb on it, and three immobile figures in a circle of light on the gable end of the village church. The first passer-by assumed they had been put there for effect – that they were statues or even paintings. But as darkness fell the images became starker and were clearly recognizable as life-sized images of the Virgin and two smaller male figures which were interpreted as St Joseph and St John. All floated some distance off the ground, as if hovering a few feet up the wall. During the several hours that they were seen none of the figures moved or spoke in any way. They behaved just like a projection of an image on to the wall.

Indeed, there are those who argue that this whole event was a hoax: magic lanterns and religious slides were available at that time. It is conceivable that someone knowingly created the image in this way, although there was no obvious building from which to do so and no reference in the evidence collected by the two subsequent church inquiries to indicate that any witness had stood in the way of a light beam and cast their shadows on to the wall. But perhaps the images were located higher off the ground than suggested, avoiding this problem.

Whatever the truth, the visions at Knock were accepted as a miracle and soon reports of the healing properties of the shrine blossomed. Clever management by the authorities secured the place's status, and the implementation in 1936 of a team of doctors to check the evidence and weed out any spurious claims furthered its reputation as a place of miracles. Today Knock has been visited by the Pope and must be the tiniest community on earth to sport its own modern international airport.

The church at Knock in 1879.

As the Sunday of the expedition approached, however, she had decided to cry off. On the Friday her kidneys had become seriously infected and she felt so ill that she actually expected to die within days. However, when Gerry arrived he persuaded her to change her mind. Her stretchered body was carefully loaded into the old ambulance, and she cursed him in good-humoured fashion as they rattled over the country roads on the 50-mile journey to Knock.

A Mother's Plea

Marion was led first into the reception ward for sick pilgrims adjacent to the basilica. Here she was well looked after, as were the many other sick people

The Shrine at Knock, County Mayo. On August 21, 1879, the Virgin Mary, St Joseph and St John the Evangelist appeared at the south gable end of the old parish church. This exterior wall is now enclosed in a vast glass box. The old church tower peers over the modern roof.

who had come that day. Nurses in old-fashioned white uniforms, used to handling very sick people at the shrine, cared for all her needs along each step of the way.

Sadie Feeley was the aid worker in charge that afternoon. Although she came from Athlone she had never met Marion before, and was shocked by her condition. 'Marion was very, very sick. She was really dying. I am not saying that to be extreme. Marion was critically ill, I'd say.'

But Marion was happy. 'When they put my stretcher in the centre, right under the statue of Our Lady which they use in the procession, I realized that this was where I wanted to be. I looked up at the statue and thought it was the most beautiful and friendly thing that I had ever seen. I felt she was just there to greet me and no one else.'

Until that moment, Marion admits, she had been thinking a great deal about dying. But the image of her family back in Athlone kept her going. Young Cora and Anthony needed her to fight on – Jimmy could not be left alone to fend for himself. 'I worried about Jimmy, because he built his whole life around me. We were one another's best friends as well as husband and wife. I was worried that when I was buried and the funeral was over and Jimmy went back home that, because he was a quiet man, people would think he did not want or need anybody. Then no one could reach out to Jimmy in his loneliness.'

This terrible emotional distress was playing on Marion's mind as she gazed up at the statue. It was at that moment that she did an extraordinary thing: she issued a heart-rending plea. 'I looked back up at the statue of Our Lady and I said to her: 'You're a mother, too. You know how I feel.' At that moment something unbelievable was set in motion.

JIMMY'S DREAM

Meanwhile, back in Athlone on that same strange day, Sunday 3 September 1989, it was also a special time for Jimmy Carroll. But in his case the reason was initially more mundane.

It was Irish hurling final day, and the match was on TV. Determined to make the most of these few hours free from his constant supervision of Marion, he put his feet up to watch the game. When the action wound down, he was overcome with tiredness and soon fell asleep. But it was not an empty sleep.

Jimmy recalls: 'I had a wonderful dream when I was asleep. I dreamt I had seen Marion walking. Then Cora came in and switched the television over from the match to cartoons and that woke me up. When I woke I was sad, after having such a lovely dream.'

It was early evening now, but still a couple of hours before Marion would be home from Knock and he would have to return to the reality of doing everything for her. But the dream had been nice while it lasted.

THE RECOVERY ROOM

Whilst Jimmy Carroll was awakening from his dream, Marion was filled with an almost indescribable sense of joy. 'When my bishop came in front of the stretcher and he blessed me I got this beautiful feeling – a magnificent feeling like a whispering breeze, telling me that if the stretcher was opened up then I could get up and walk. I remember thinking to myself – hold on, Marion. You've got more sense than getting ideas like this. I'll wait until I go home and tell Jim. He'll definitely think I've gone nutty.'

The ceremonies and the blessing of the sick had ended. Marion was now returned to the recovery room where the sick were given refreshment and time to prepare for their journey home. With the pilgrimage that day were Dr John O'Meara and his wife Nuala. At this time she came over to talk to Marion. The two women had known one another since Marion's childhood, when she had attended the same class at school as Nuala O'Meara's daughter. The doctor's wife explains what happened next, 'Marion looked ill to me. She was absolutely prone on that stretcher. There was no movement at all. It was then that she said to me that she had felt happy during the ceremonies and would I open her straps. I was surprised at that and said, "Marion, I'm not a nurse".'

However, Nuala went to find a nurse and convey this unexpected request. Maureen Rafferty, who came over in response, confirms that Marion was clearly ill. 'I said, "You know, Marion, you cannot walk." But she said that she felt she could. I think she told me that she had a burning in her feet. I just thought that maybe she had been a long time lying on the stretcher and that the straps were tight. So I undid the straps for her. Then she wanted me to take the blankets off. I took them off her and she tried to move her legs off the stretcher.' Maureen and Nuala recall trying to help Marion, but she resisted their efforts. They did, however, guide her into an upright position, itself an unexpected feat.

Marion describes the scene: 'I had no control over what happened next. Nurse Rafferty opened the stretcher and my two legs swung out and I stood up straight. I wasn't even a bit stiff after all those years, and Sister Antonio noticed that I was holding my head myself without the collar and that I was using my arms and hands and that my speech was perfect. But when I stood up at Knock it had nothing to do with walking or moving. I was so full of joy and peace and a love that has no end. It was like looking directly into the sun and the rays came towards me and I got all the gifts of that joy – the great peace and great love.'

Somehow, without explanation, and to the astonishment of the doctor's wife and the watching nurse, Marion had cast aside thirteen years of serious disability and was walking without aid as if it were the most natural thing in the world. Her face beamed with the inner peace that she was feeling.

The shrine at Knock has received many distinguished visitors. In June 1993 Mother Teresa of Calcutta recited sections of the rosary in front of huge crowds.

Robert Gutherman and his late mother Beatrice meeting the Pope after the beatification ceremony for Katharine Drexel (see Chapter 4).

Inside the shrine are three tall white statues of Carrara marble bought in Italy; an alter, lamb and encircling angels depicting the scene witnessed in 1879.

MIRACLE OR REMISSION?

After the journey home to Athlone, Anne Flanagan and Gerry Glynn helped Marion to clamber out of the ambulance. They were greeted by Jimmy bringing the wheelchair outside to take her indoors. At first he did not suspect that anything was amiss, but it was not long before the truth dawned upon him.

Marion remembers clearly the scene as she met Jimmy at the door that evening: 'He said, "Well Marion, how's Knock?" I said it was all right, but why would anybody bother going down there? I got into the wheelchair because that's the only thing I knew. We came into our home and Jimmy sat down by the patio doors and I stood up and said, "Look, Jim, I can walk!" He said, "Oh God, don't, don't!" But I went over and put my arms around him and he got down on his knees and started to thank the Lord and he was crying.' Jimmy has no doubt that she was the recipient of a miracle sent from God. 'It had to be. She has never looked back, never an ache or pain since.'

So was it truly a miracle or was there some medical explanation? Those who were present that day have no doubt. Ambulance driver Gerry Glynn confirms: 'She was really a sick woman. I felt myself, well she cannot have a whole lot of time left and I wondered whether it would be a waste of time bringing her at all. But we carried on.'

As for what he witnessed: 'It was a miracle, all right. Definitely. People with MS will get a remission from time to time, maybe for a few months, but not for anything like the time that Marion has.' Six years have now passed since that Sunday and Marion Carroll is still walking as freely as ever. Maureen Rafferty says, from her perspective as a nurse, 'I thought then – and I think still – that I witnessed a miracle, because I had seen Marion on the stretcher and I knew that she had paralysis and I saw her walking. So I thought that was a miracle.' Knock aid worker Sadie Feeley was even more certain: 'I would have no hesitation. I'd say it was a miracle. I felt when I was looking upon it that I was very privileged to be at Knock that day.'

Not everyone, however, can accept miracles without question. Dr Diarmuid Murray heads the Medical Bureau attached to Knock and his responsibility is to check the facts in as much detail as possible. He feels that her case deserves a thorough study. 'If you arrived in Knock on a stretcher, totally incapacitated, and literally took up your bed and walked home, just as in the biblical story, it does require looking at very closely.'

However, the key medical question is whether Marion really ever had multiple sclerosis. Dr Murray agrees: 'She had many of the features consistent with the disease, therefore for someone to make such a dramatic and instant cure immediately raises medical interest.' The first step in the process of authentication is simply to watch and do nothing, basically observing how Marion progresses. As the doctor points out, today 'multiple sclerosis is unfortunately one of those conditions where people can get remissions and then after a period of years begin to relapse again; although I must say that six years is quite a long time for that.' But he warns that there have been cases 'of people who have been cured where we found that in point of fact they have not been suffering from what they thought they were'.

Once the doctor is confident that Marion's cure is permanent, a formal medical commission will be set up to investigate the evidence. Dr Murray says: 'We are in the process of doing that now – sending all the details to medical experts around the country. Any doctor is welcome to write to us and obtain the facts and make his or her own comments on the matter.' When collated, these comments will be discussed at a meeting to which specialists will be invited, as will Marion herself, and which will decide

Opposite *Pope John Paul II blessing a child in the Basilica at Knock, September 30, 1979.*

Marion Carroll (centre) with her husband and daughter in front of the statue of the Virgin Mary at Knock.

whether to continue with further observation or pass the affair on to the church for further assessment.

As Dr Murray points out: 'Orthodox doctors are not trained to think in terms of miracles. It is not our function to decide whether something is miraculous or not. The doctors must only try to explain the person's cure. If we cannot, then we hand the case over to the bishop of the diocese in which the claimant lives.'

All that Dr Murray can really say is that it will be left to the Church to determine what took place. 'Marion has fulfilled in a sense all three conditions: namely that her cure was instant, it was complete and now, six years later, it has been maintained. Indeed Marion has gone from strength to strength.'

A GIFT FROM GOD?

The Carrolls' priest, Father Tom O'Reilly, recalls how he first heard the wonderful news. 'The last time I saw Marion was the week before. I felt it was just a question of time. She was in the terminal stage of her illness. She wanted me to be with her at the end.' Then Jimmy sent for him and he came to the obvious conclusion. 'I thought that she had died, or that she was dying, at least. I just took it for granted that she was dying and wanted me to be there.' But, of course, Marion was not dying and to this priest her recovery was astonishing. 'It was just as spectacular and sensational as any of the great gospel miracles.'

After doing the rounds of all her specialists and getting signed off by them, Marion still smiles when she recalls their expressions, no less stunned than that of her priest. 'I don't think they knew what to say,' she admits. 'Can you imagine something happening in your life that has never happened before – one that there is no explanation for? I could picture them, in their own minds, trying to find an explanation. It must have been very hard on them.'

Pilgrim's plea before the altar

MARION'S family are convinced that a miracle saved her life and cured her of Multiple Sclerosis.

Marion only agreed to go with friends on the pilgrimage to Knock on September 3, 1989 because she thought it would give her family a break.

She was brought to the shrine in an ambulance and carried into the church on a stretcher.

"I was placed under the statue of Our Lady of Knock," said Marion.

"I didn't have the heart to pray. I ˑ aid to Mary 'You'...

"He fell on his knees, crying and thanking the Lord," said Marion.

"Jimmy told me he had prayed for God to take him and cure me. Now it was my turn to comfort him."

While Jimmy was crying in Marion's arms, her daughter Cora came into the house and was shocked to see her mother standing.

"She gaped at me," recalls Marion.

"It was unforgettabḷ· ·beautiful to walk over ˑˑ ...

An extract from Sunday Life *(Belfast), December 4, 1994.*

So what does Marion believe happened to her that day beneath the statue in Knock? She remembers how people kept asking why she had been cured. Was she a saint?

'But I'm not. I'm just an ordinary person. The Lord is the only one who knows, so I started asking, "Jesus, why me?". One night during our family rosary I got my answer. My cure – my healing at Knock – does not belong to me. This is a special gift to you and all the people of the world to let you know that Jesus and Mary are there. Life is pretty hard at times and sometimes we actually need to feel, touch and see God's love, because we are so human. That is why I am sitting here now talking. It is not my gift. It is the gift to the people – but why he chose me I do not know.'

4

THE MAKING OF A MIRACLE

What is a miracle? It can be many things to many different people, of course. But so far as the Catholic Church is concerned there are very strict criteria which govern the decision. Indeed, the process by which an event is decreed to be a miracle is one of the most thorough that can be imagined. Few cases which are undeniably strange – but true – are subjected to such rigorous analysis.

As a consequence, anything which receives official sanction must be regarded as serious evidence for the supernatural. For a remarkable story to pass through all the barriers placed in its way and still be regarded as inexplicable means that it has to be something quite extraordinary. That is certainly a fair description of the experience that befell Robert Gutherman from Philadelphia, USA. In 1974 Robert was rushed to St Christopher's Hospital suffering from acute pains in the side of his head. At first it may have seemed like simple earache, but it was to prove a lot more dangerous than that.

THE WORST PAIN OF MY LIFE

Robert was just a fourteen-year-old boy in 1974, but even now, as a father with a child of his own, he recalls the searing pain that would not go away. 'It hurt so much that we used to put heat on my ear. I remember my mother boiling water and putting it in a hot water bottle, and then I put a towel over that. It is the worst pain I have ever had in my whole life.'

The trouble got gradually worse and was not responding to any treatment at home. Eventually, the Guthermans felt they should take Robert to a children's hospital in the city. At St Christopher's Dr Myles Turtz, a specialist in ear disease recognized the seriousness of the problem: Robert had an acute mastoid infection.

The specialist says: 'The standard assessment was to do the clinical evaluation, take the history, do a series of x-rays, a run of hearing tests – to get as much information as we could.' Robert was unable to hear out of one of his ears, and surgery was needed. Only when he was operated on was the full extent of Robert's illness discovered.

Dr Turtz reports: 'We had a sense of what we would find, but when I got in there what I had not anticipated was that the extent of the disease would be such that all landmarks to guide me in the surgery would be unavailable.'

In fact, the infection which had previously been diagnosed had caused extensive injury. It had eaten away at the bone linking the ear to the brain, exposing part of the covering of the brain. If this had progressed unchecked for much longer meningitis and even death could have swiftly followed. The situation was so bad that Dr Turtz had to abandon all hope of helping Robert recover his hearing. 'There was so much disease that I made the judgement that the best I could do was to clean it up,' the doctor concluded sadly.

PRAYING FOR ROBERT

The main concern of the doctor when he first went to see Robert and his parents on the ward after the operation was to assure himself that the boy had not been left with any facial paralysis or other serious after-effects. He was grateful to find that his patient had not deteriorated, but could not anticipate that he would be much improved. 'I wanted to make sure that the parents had a very realistic view of what to expect. So when I went down to make my rounds with my team I told them that in my opinion – I had looked in there – I had seen this awful disease and had made a judgement not to proceed further. I anticipated zero return of hearing on the basis of what I had seen.'

It was natural that a devoutly Catholic family such as the Guthermans would pray for their son. After all, even though Dr Turtz believed that he had saved any immediate threat to Robert's life, the fears still persisted. George Gutherman, Robert's father, explains: 'Every night after dinner we sat at table and we would say the rosary. Then we had prayer cards from the convent. We did that before Robert even got sick. So we just kept it up and went down to the hospital and took these prayer cards with us, and we gave them out to different people we met and asked them to pray for Robert. We

From the family album: Robert Gutherman with his mother Beatrice.

had a prayer card on the bedside table, but Robert was too sick to be praying, so my wife and I did that.'

Indeed, Beatrice Gutherman was allowed to stay by her son's bed almost constantly in a form of prayer vigil. She had also consulted the local convent where Robert had served as an altar boy. The nuns here had agreed to pray for his recovery and suggested they should all dedicate their prayers to the order's founder – Mother Katharine Drexel. That was to prove a monumental decision.

WHO'S CALLING MY NAME?

After recovering from the anaesthetic Robert Gutherman has a curious recollection. 'One of the things I remember most vividly was waking up in the middle of the night and someone in the hallway was hollering "Bobby!". My mother stayed the night with me in hospital and I woke up and she was

A REMARKABLE WOMAN

Born in the mid-nineteenth century, Katharine Drexel was the daughter of Francis and Hannah Drexel, a very wealthy Philadelphia couple. Her mother died soon after her birth and two years later her father married Emma Bouvier. Katharine's new stepmother was a deeply spiritual woman who raised her family almost as if they were monks and nuns, teaching them to live with reverence. They were urged to be of service to humanity.

This upbringing formed a marked contrast with Francis Drexel's extraordinary wealth – he owned three banks and was a multi-millionaire. Part of his fortune was eventually inherited by Katharine, of course, but she had been taught not to use it for personal gain and wanted to put it to some good purpose.

Eventually she decided to forsake material pleasures and chose to enter a convent under the guidance of her mentor, Bishop O'Connor. Her vast wealth was invested and the phenomenal sums of interest that it generated were used to set up a spiritual mission to develop the work of the order.

Katharine died in 1955 when almost a hundred years old and her money has continued to benefit the order,

Mother Katharine Drexel, foundress of the Sisters of the Blessed Sacrament.

which now has sixty-five missions in twenty-one states of the USA. Not surprisingly, the nuns who continue her work greatly admire her dedication and have urged the Vatican to let her have official recognition from the Catholic Church. However, to be considered for sainthood one thing was lacking from Katharine's inspirational story – a miracle that could be attributed to her intervention. This is why the nuns whom Beatrice Gutherman consulted suggested that her prayers for Robert be dedicated to the memory of Katharine Drexel.

sort of dozing in the chair, and so I asked her who was calling my name. She said nobody was – they were calling for somebody in the hallway.'

Of course, the fact that Robert claimed to be hearing distant sounds suggested to his mother that perhaps his hearing was normal, despite what Dr Turtz had said. Robert adds, 'The next morning, when the doctor came in, my mother told him that I could hear and I remember him looking at us and saying, "No." He had already told her that there was too much damage and that I would never be able to hear out of that ear.' However, Robert continued to experience things that suggested the opposite. He had been bought a pocket watch as a present, and its ticking was so loud he had to put it away in the bedside cabinet. He told Dr Turtz about this as well. 'I don't really think he believed us,' Robert points out. 'But I did hear it ticking.'

Dr Turtz notes that it is not uncommon for patients with hearing loss to believe that they can hear out of the injured ear. 'There is something called the placebo effect. You are imagining that you can hear out of that ear because you are wishing intensely that it will happen. On the basis of what I had seen I did not expect it to really happen, but Bobby kept saying, "Yes, I am hearing." '

So, a few days after leaving hospital, Robert returned to the ear specialist for an audiometry test to see exactly what was taking place. 'This is not something we normally do,' the doctor explained. 'The ear was still a mess, but on the first audiometry test the hearing was improved. It was not normal, but it was improved and that came as a little bit of a surprise to me.' It was not to be the last shock the doctor would receive.

THE TRIBUNAL

Within a few more days Robert's hearing had returned to normal. He describes the scene in Dr Turtz's office at this discovery. 'He was looking into my ear and my mother was sitting across from us and he was saying to her, "I can't believe what I am seeing. His body is reconstructing anatomy." My mother asked him what that meant and he said, "His body is healing itself."'

Armed with such astonishing news, and in no doubt about what had happened, the family decided to report the success to the Church. 'It had to be a miracle,' George Gutherman insists to this day. 'This doctor is a world-renowned children's doctor and he said that our boy, our baby boy, would never hear because two bones were missing from his ear. Yet when he examined him again he said they were there – they were reconstructing themselves.'

Robert reports, 'We left the doctor's office that day and we drove directly to the Sisters of the Blessed Sacrament. We explained to the sister that we had what we believed was a miracle through Mother Katharine Drexel's intercession.' Sister Ruth Catherine remembers that visit. 'Everyone was thrilled,' she reports. 'Robert seemed to be cured, but it still needed to be certified. We cautioned them not to proclaim it to the neighbourhood – to keep it within the family, because if something like that is named as miraculous by the people and announced to others it is negated and will not be investigated by the Church.'

The only proper course of action now was to launch a tribunal to discover whether Robert really had been cured by miraculous intervention. The Archdiocese of Philadelphia set about resolving this question.

A PHILADELPHIA STORY

Monsignor Martino explains the process by which an inquiry into such a miracle is set up. 'The purpose is to make sure that everyone is clear that this is a very serious event and not the product of someone's imagination or something that happened accidentally. Indeed, it is something that is inexplicable – ie the medical personnel cannot explain what happened – and there is an element of divine intervention.' Of course, this is easier said than done, as the Monsignor agrees. 'Since none of that is easy to see with the naked eye, it is important for people to have the assurance of a serious inquiry.'

The tribunal sits almost like a court, with a judge, notary and devil's advocate leading the questioning of key witnesses. The job of the tribunal is to determine whether there is a natural explanation for the cure. If not, they make the recommendation of a miracle to Rome. Of course, ultimately, only the Pope can confer this status.

Any investigation into a case such as Robert's has to establish two things: first, that a medical mystery has occurred and secondly, that prayer or intervention by God was a direct factor in the alleged recovery.

As the Monsignor points out, 'The church has a great stake in making sure that absolutely clear judicial procedures are nailed down and followed scrupulously from the beginning to the end. Should there be any failure on the part of the tribunal to observe the Church's rules, the Vatican will not proceed any further with the investigation.'

In addition, time is often a factor. It took many years for the Robert Gutherman case to be investigated, largely because its allegedly miraculous instigator, Katharine Drexel, was not granted the status of being 'of heroic virtue' until 1986. This is a prerequisite for the exploration of a miracle. Katharine Drexel was well loved in Philadelphia, so there was intense interest in her potential saintliness. Much of the city was drawn in by the investigation. The study of Robert's case began in 1987 – some fourteen years after his dramatic recovery. The time had arrived to determine what had happened – in the eyes of the Church.

Vatican City. The facade of St Peter's.

THE SEARCH FOR TRUTH

Despite being not a Catholic but a Jew, Dr Turtz was happy to give evidence in the imposing panelled tribunal room. He sat at an old, heavy table, surrounded by clergy.

'It was very much like a court room,' he noted. Calmly the doctor explained what he had witnessed, answering the questions of the priest whose task was to serve as devil's advocate. Dr Turtz told them plainly what his medical position was. 'I have no explanation. I opened a diseased area. I carefully, over hours of time, tried to clean that disease out, and when I closed the skin I left a lot of disease. So how the Gutherman child got the result that he did is unexplainable to me. I have done these kinds of cases hundreds, if not thousands, of times and I have never seen this happen.' He added, to sum up his amazement, 'If you ask me what did I do to get that outcome, I will tell you that I did not do anything.'

Dr Felice Santore had the role of providing independent medical advice to the panel. He remembers when he first saw the papers on the case. 'It was really unbelievable because I had done dozens of the same type of operation, and to get a result that quickly and that amazingly was almost unbelievable. Following the surgery Dr Turtz could not find the ossicles – little bones in the ear without which you cannot have any type of hearing whatsoever. The results were so stupendous that we could not believe that this boy did not have these little ossicles working.' He agrees that it is possible that Dr Turtz simply missed seeing the ossicles, but finds this difficult to conceive given the surgeon's expertise.

In the end Dr Santore concluded, 'As a Catholic physician I can feel that it was a miraculous recovery. We, as non-clergy, do not have the right to deal in miracles, but to the best of our knowledge we felt that it was something that we could not explain.'

However, the investigation needed more than this. So they brought in the services of Professor Louis Lowry, one of America's most prestigious authorities on ear disease. His investigation used the most sophisticated techniques available, which were by now much more advanced than those to which Dr Turtz had had access in 1974. These showed conclusively that the ossicles were present in Robert Gutherman's ear and were acting normally.

Had they been present all along, and had Dr Turtz simply missed seeing them? After stressing the reliability and expertise of the surgeon, the Professor says, 'It is possible that they were there, but doubtful. I just think that probably Dr Turtz's description of what he saw is accurate.' He later elaborated, 'It is possible that a surgeon such as Dr Turtz could miss the ossicles. Possible, but it is extremely unlikely because of the nature of the surgery.'

So had they grown back after the surgery? Professor Lowry comments, 'Well, I guess you could say yes, if you believed in miracles. But, as far as I know, I have never seen any grow back physiologically. I would not think it was possible.'

Professor Lowry points out that he is not qualified to judge miracles. He can only describe what he observed.

WHEN IN ROME

The tribunal were satisfied with their investigation and recommended the recognition of Katharine Drexel's involvement to the Vatican. In 1987, after secret deliberations, the decision was reached and she was put on the road towards sainthood. Robert Gutherman's cure was decreed to be miraculous. The following year Robert and his parents flew to Rome to be blessed by the Pope and to take part in a beatification ceremony for Katharine Drexel within the Vatican (see photograph opposite page 49). They were immensely proud to make this journey, especially Beatrice, who was desperately ill from cancer.

Despite the temptation to ask for another miracle, to save her life, the Guthermans did not do so. Beatrice has since died. George Gutherman

A scene depicting the canonisation of Saints by Clement XI in 1712.

explains, 'A lot of people said, "Why don't you pray that your wife will be cured from cancer?" But she said that would not be the way. If God wanted it, he would have her cured. Whatever God wants will happen.'

Perhaps such devotion explains why the Guthermans were granted their one miracle.

PART THREE

PAST LIVES & NEAR DEATH EXPERIENCES

Do you remember the last time that you died?

Such a question seems absurd. But is it, in the face of testimony you are about to confront? For there are people who say they have died – and lived to tell the tale.

Some, under the influence of hypnosis, become somebody else, deep in the past, reliving their lives – and their deaths – in chilling detail.

Surely this must be illusion? Such memories are fantasies invented by the mind. If you search for evidence to support the claim, then it will simply disappear. Or will it?

The reports of those who have had near death experiences are equally revealing. But surely their experiences too can be nothing more than delusions brought about by fear of imminent death and oblivion?

But what if this delusion is coherent? What if this delusion saves their life?

Perhaps there is more to death than you have imagined.

5

A MAN OUT OF TIME

To travel in time is one of mankind's greatest dreams; to live forever is perhaps our deepest yearning. There is one phenomenon that combines both these ambitions and, if proven, would establish that there is life after death. That phenomenon is the concept of past lives: the idea that inside every human being, like some animated version of a Russian doll, are many other selves, each one a distinct personality with its own history from birth to death. These 'other yous' may be buried ever deeper by each new life we lead; and, of course, the only conscious reality we can be aware of is the one we live right now.

This may sound ridiculous to our modern, Western way of thinking, yet billions of people around the world believe it to be established fact. Western society is out of phase with those members of the human race who incorporate reincarnation into their religious beliefs. But even here opinions are changing, with a rising fascination in research that probes past life memories.

So are these other lives, often located way back in the past, a secret part of us all? Do they go on haunting the darkest corners of our mind until they are snatched back to attention? If the experiences of Ray Bryant from Reading are taken seriously, that seems a very definite possibility. For he has offered what many paranormal researchers consider to be the most astounding evidence that past lives are more than just a product of the imagination.

A VOICE ON THE RADIO

For investigator Andrew Selby it began in 1979, when he heard a stranger's voice on the radio. The man was speaking in soothing northern tones about the oddest things. Joe Keeton was claiming that as a hypnotherapist he had regressed countless people back to a time when they remembered being somebody else. They told their stories in the first person – as if they were really living through these experiences from centuries before they were born. Perhaps they were recalling previous lives, when their soul or spirit inhabited different bodies.

Here, thought Andrew, was a remarkable mystery to be solved, so he contacted the radio station and asked for further details. Eventually a letter arrived from an address in the north of England, in which the hypnotist suggested that his enthusiastic correspondent should start up a group in the London area. Andrew readily agreed to hold monthly meetings at his home. Joe Keeton himself would come along and one by one regress those who attended to see if they could be coaxed towards memories of a distant time and place.

'We normally would have about fifteen,' Andrew explains. 'We don't like to have too many as it gets a bit crowded and becomes more like a spectacle. Once Joe has put a person under hypnosis he asks everyone to start questioning, and we try to do it in a natural way.'

Unless you are gentle, he adds, the subjects tend to freeze up. Getting information about a past life is rather like extracting a tooth – it is a slow and delicate operation that should not be hurried, and it can take many sessions before any progress is made. With some people nothing ever happens, but most find strange images floating inside their heads, and these can become the basis for a full-blown past life memory. That was the way of it with Reading journalist Ray Bryant, whose story began just like any other but was destined to lead to far stranger things.

JUST A JOB TO DO

In 1979 Ray was sent on a typical assignment by the newspaper on which he worked. He was asked to interview an unusual Merseyside man, Joe Keeton, who had just published a book called *Encounters with the Past*, in which he claimed that he could uncover people's previous lives by putting them under hypnosis.

When Ray went to the book launch it was just another job to do. But by the end of the day it had become a personal fascination that would not let him go. 'Joe held a session to demonstrate his methods to journalists at the launch,' Ray reports. He told them that about 90 per cent of subjects were suggestible and could be put into a hypnotic state. Ray volunteered.

'Fortunately, I was able to be hypnotized and, although nobody at that session actually regressed beyond their own life, what I saw was enough to get me very interested.'

Joe recommended that he visit Andrew Selby's group – perhaps to write a story about their work in southern England, then still in its earliest days. Ray leaped at the chance.

REGRESSION

Before he visited Andrew's house, Ray had no clear idea about what to expect. 'I suppose I had, like many people, a rather fanciful notion of what regression was like – something like the spirit leaving the body and finding a new life somewhere.' Now he knows it is far more complicated than that.

He told me when I interviewed him in 1986, not long after his case came to the attention of the research community: 'I would not say that I actually believed in reincarnation. I liked the idea, but I imagined people regressing back to glamorous lives as highwaymen, pilots, smugglers or princes. Nothing mundane.' That thought, too, was soon to be dispelled.

At first Ray simply observed others in the small group and wrote his piece on their activities for the local paper. His few personal attempts at regression led him nowhere, for a reason that Andrew explains. 'Ray actually had a mental block, which was basically stopping him from regressing. It was a nightmare of a giant spider when he was aged about six or seven.' The reporter could not go past this barrier until he was guided through the trauma by Joe Keeton and could then relive his emergence from the womb. As Andrew recalls: 'It was a number of months or even a year before Ray was able to regress beyond his own birth. When he did we started getting some responses.'

In fact the first image that Ray saw, as he told me in 1986, was very specific. 'Curiously enough, it was nothing more interesting than a bandstand.' He had no idea where this military-style building might be, and it was some time before he learned the truth. The memory seemed to belong to another time, to a man whom he could only first identify as 'Reuben St ___'.

Like so many cases that the London group had studied, this one seemed doomed to offer vague images and no hard data – nothing that could be verified. But this pessimism was unwarranted, and Ray Bryant's case was to prove revolutionary.

47th REGIMENT OF FOOT

NO.	NAME	RANK	CASUALTY	DATE
3266	Hodgins Michael	Pte.	Killed	7-6-55
2047	Hood George	Pte.	Killed	7-6-55
2785	Kelly John	Pte.	Killed	7-6-55
2758	Kelly Patrick	Pte.	Killed	7-6-55
3063	Kelly Stephen	Pte.	Killed	7-6-55
—	Long John	Pte.	Killed	7-6-55
2560	Murphy John	Pte.	Killed	7-6-55
3311	Murray Charles	Pte.	Killed	7-6-55
2728	Newton John	Pte.	Killed	7-6-55
3315	Noonan Michael	Pte.	Killed	7 6-55
3386	O'Neil Hugh	Pte.	Killed	7-6-55
2848	Shackey Patrick	Pte.	Killed	7-6-55
2997	Whealan Edward	Pte.	Killed	7-6-55
2868	White Michael	Pte.	Killed	7-6-55
	Villiers J.	Major	W/Sv	7-6-55
	Lowndes J. H.	Capt.	W/Sv	7-6-55
	Hunter F. W. F.	Capt.	W/Sv	7-6-55
	Irby J. J. C.	Lieut.	W/D	7-6-55
2064	Beatson Donald	Sergt.	W/Sv	7-6-55
1784	Stafford Reuben	Sergt.	W/Sl	7-6-55
2633	Grant William	Corpl.	W/Sl	7-6-55
1377	Lang George	Corpl.	W/Sl	7-6-55
3199	O'Loughlin John		W/Sl	7-6-55
3409			W/Sl	7-6-55
1674			W/Sl	7-6-55
3396			W/Sl	7-6-55
3201			W/Sv	7-6-55

Above *A page from the register of troops of the 47th Regiment of Foot killed or injured in the Crimean War.*

Left *Major J Villiers, who was wounded in command of the 47th during the successful assault on the Quarries, Sebastopol, 7 June 1855 – the same day that Reuben Stafford was himself injured.*

A SOLDIER OF THE QUEEN

Keeton and Selby began to get the feeling that the period in question was the Crimean War of 1853-6, and that the mysterious Reuben St__ had fought on the British side in this conflict against Russia.

Andrew Selby remembers: 'I was down at the Guildhall Library looking into another regression case and was not getting anywhere. So I thought I would look and see if I could find anything on the Crimean War.'

Andrew took out a large blue volume that listed all the casualties in this war. 'I did not have much to go on – just that Ray had told us it was a Lancashire regiment. So I started looking through the book and I nearly fell off my chair. There in front of me was this Reuben Stafford in a Lancashire regiment – the 47th. He was wounded slightly in the hand. I was absolutely amazed and phoned Joe minutes afterwards.'

The investigation group took the decision to delve as far as possible into Reuben Stafford's obscure history and learn whatever they could. However, they purposely chose not to share these details with Ray Bryant. They wanted him to tell the story in his (or Reuben's) own words, so that they could compare what he was saying against the truth that they were uncovering.

TRICKS THAT FAILED

When Ray Bryant described Reuben's birth in 1827, he did so in a curious way. Ray explains: 'He was born in Brighton, and there's another interesting point. I answered with the name of Brighthelmstone – which is the old name for Brighton.' Ray admits that he knew Brighton had once been called by this other name, but pointed out that it would not have been natural for him to have used that word.

As the regression sessions progressed, Ray's accent noticeably changed and thickened. His gentle West Country burr took on the characteristics of a working man from Lancashire – the area to which Reuben moved and where he grew up before joining the Army. Andrew Selby, like the other members of his group, noticed the dramatic differences between Ray and Reuben. 'Ray is quite an easy-going sort of fellow and Reuben is a much more bombastic type with quite a different manner. It is noticeable when you see Ray under hypnosis.'

During the process, Ray was curiously detached. 'Seeing these events in Reuben's life is a rather strange experience, because it is rather like being a witness and at the same time a participant. It is like watching a television

OF THE EVENTS OF THE WAR. 1855.

June 1.—Admiral Dundas was joined near Cronstadt by the French fleet

„ 3.—The Allied Admirals reconnoitred the north side of Cronstadt

„ „ The Allied Squadron in the Sea of Azoff fired the stores and government buildings of Taganrog, in the face of 3,000 Russian soldiers. A war steamer of the enemy, also, was destroyed

„ 4.—The Allied Squadron in the Sea of Azoff proceeded to Mariopol, where it destroyed extensive grain stores and the public buildings

„ „ Anapa, the last of the Russian forts on the Circassian coast of the Black Sea, was burnt and abandoned by its garrison. The ruins were visited by Admirals Stewart and Charnier.

„ 5.—A General Order announced to the Allied Armies the triumphs of the fleets in the Sea of Azoff

„ „ The cutter of a British man-of-war, while landing some Russian prisoners at Hango, without notice previously given, and with a flag of truce irregularly displayed, was fired into, and several men killed. The affair was, at first, greatly exaggerated and misrepresented in England, where it occasioned much excitement. A correspondence took place concerning it between Admiral Dundas and the Russian authorities

„ 6.—Several thousand quarters of wheat were burnt by the Allied Squadron at the little town of Gheisk

„ „ The French and English opened a furious fire against the external works of Sebastopol, and obtained a superiority over that of the enemy on several points

„ 7.—The French assaulted and captured the famous work known as "the Mamelon." In their enthusiasm they assaulted the terrible Malakhoff Tower behind it, but were repulsed with much loss. The English assaulted and took the "Quarries;" a murderous fight was maintained the whole night

The French established themselves securely in the Mamelon, which they gave programme and being involved in it at the same time. You see the scenery. You see the action. You see the people around you that in life you don't know. But you know what is happening all of the time.'

Possessing increasing data about Reuben's life and the Crimean War provided the group with an opportunity, as Andrew points out. 'We have tried to trick him. We have tried to trap him and to break his story.' Ray admits there were one or two minor problems, as it was difficult translating from Reuben to himself. Sometimes he was not deep enough into the hypnotic state and his conscious mind fought to supply what it thought were better (but erroneous) replies. But in the most important features he held firm. 'The part with the military record we have not been able to break,' Andrew agrees, 'even though we put in all sorts of sneaky tricks.'

A VERY ORDINARY LIFE

Reuben described fighting inside a quarry against grey-coated Russians with flat hats sporting green bands. The details were vivid and real. Then he told about his injury: 'Going through Reuben's wounding was rather an odd experience the first time because, whilst I was aware that he was feeling something very sharp and sudden, I was not aware of any pain myself.' Only after the hypnosis session during which he re-experienced that last battle was Ray Bryant told about Reuben's injury. Then all the sensations he had gone through during the regression fell into place.

After being wounded he was tended by a group of nurses, and when asked under hypnosis who they were he replied, 'Florie's ladies'. This was the name popularly given to the nursing unit taken to the Crimea by Florence Nightingale.

Invalided back home, Reuben became a colour sergeant at the barracks in Fulwood, Preston, before leaving the army in 1865. Evidence of his humble military career has been successfully traced in the archives. There is no bandstand at Fulwood today, but records confirm that in the mid-nineteenth century one stood precisely where Reuben described it to be.

Eventually Reuben moved south to London and lived with his son who was an articled clerk. After a family dispute, however, Reuben set up home on his

Opposite above *A catalogue of events of the war during early June 1855.*
Opposite below *Headquarters of the 47th (Lancashire) Regiment in the Crimea. The group includes three visiting cavalrymen.*

Canada ℓℓ 27ᵗʰ March

25257 HER
MAJESTY'S   47ᵗʰ   REG.

OF   Foot

Whereof   General Sir J. S. Kennedy KCB   is Colonel.

[Place and Date] Hamilton W. 23 March   1865.

PROCEEDINGS OF A REGIMENTAL BOARD, held this day, in conformity to the
Articles of War, for the purpose of verifying and recording the Services, Conduct, Character, and
cause of Discharge of No. 1784, Color Sergeant Rueben Stafford
of the Regiment above-mentioned.

President.
Lieut. Col. Villiers

Capt. Straton   Members.   Capt. Newman

THE BOARD having examined and compared the Regimental Records, the
Soldier's Book, and such other Documents as appeared to them to be necessary, report that after
making every deduction required by Her Majesty's Regulations, the Service up to this day,
which he is entitled to reckon, amounts to 21 years, 1 days, as shown by the
detailed Statement on the 2nd page; during which period he served abroad 10 7/12 years, viz.:

at Ionian Islands 2/11 years, Malta 2 years, Turkey 6/12 years,
in Crimea 1 9/12 years, Gibraltar 3 months, Canada 3 5/12 years;

and further, that his DISCHARGE is proposed in consequence of having Completed

[Here state whether—Completion of
period, at his own request, or as unfit
for further Service.]

Upwards of twenty one Years actual
Service, at his own request with Pension

With regard to the CHARACTER and CONDUCT of Colr. Sergeant Rueben
Stafford   the Board have to report that upon reference to the
Defaulter's Book, and by the Parole testimony that has been given, it appears that he

has been a very good Soldier

[Insert opposite—the man's Character, the number of Good Conduct
Badges in his possession, and all
Badges of Merit, or gallant conduct in
the Field, conferred upon him.]

He is in possession of the Crimean Medal with
clasps for Inkerman and Sebastopol, the Turkish
Crimean Medal, the Medal for good Conduct
and long Service — and was in possession of
two good Conduct Badges when promoted
Corporal.

[Insert the number of times his
Name appears in the Defaulter's Book,
and that he has been tried by Court
Martial.

N° 1784 C Sejt Ruben Stafford being asked to what date he has been paid, answered, that his Account is balanced up to the latest period required by the Regulations; and being further asked whether he has any claim on the Regiment for Arrears of PAY, ALLOWANCES, or CLOTHING, answered, that he has received all just demands, from his entry into the Service up to the *present date* and in confirmation therefore, affixes his signature hereto.

I acknowledge this to be true. *R Stafford*

Witness *Glid Daverush 47 Regt*

Commanding the Company to which he belongs.

THE Board have ascertained that *C Sejeant Ruben Stafford's* Soldier's Book is correctly balanced, and signed by the Officer Commanding his Company, and they declare, that they have impartially inquired into, and faithfully reported upon, all the matters brought before them, in accordance with the Regulations and Instructions issued by Her Majesty's Orders.

C C Villun Lt Col Majr 47 Regt President.

Menes de Stratton Capt 47 Regt Members.

W Newman Capt 47 Regt

Detailed Statement of the Services of *Color Sajeant Ruben Stafford*

		Period of Service in each Rank	Amount of

No. *1784 C Sejt Reuben Stafford* referred to in the preceding pages, by Trade a *Laborer* was born in the Parish of *Brightelmston* near the Town of *Brightelmston* in the County of *Sussex* and attested for the *47* Regt. at *Brighton* in the County of *Sussex* on the *22 March 1844* at the Age of *20 Years*

His final description, &c., when discharged from the Service, at _____

this ___ day of ___ 18__.
Age *41 Years*
Height *5* Feet *9* Inches,
Complexion *Fair*
Eyes *Blue*
Hair *Light*
Trade *Laborer*
Marks or Scars upon the face, or other parts of the body *Wounded on left hand*

Intended Place of Residence *Kingston Camden Nel*

Opposite and above *Various of Reuben Stafford's army documents found in the archives of the 47th Regiment.*

A FAMILY TREE OF PAST LIVES

People who are regressed many times rarely go back to just one past life. Ray Bryant is no exception. Amongst his other lives which have been partially investigated (in some cases he is unclear about dates) he describes the following:

- 1790s: his final years as Wilfred, a coachman on the London-to-Bath route who did little other than get drunk at the Swan Inn near Didcot (not far from where Ray Bryant lives today).
- Early 1800s: a life as Elizabeth, a cleaning girl who died quite young.
- 1827-79: Reuben Stafford.
- Early 1900s: Robert Sawyer, a poor Essex peasant.
- Around 1920: a young girl, the daughter of a rich family, who died at the age of five.
- Then, in 1939, Ray Bryant was born.

It is interesting to note how the gaps between lives have been decreasing in line with the rapid rise in population during the twentieth century. Is this, as sceptics suggest, because modern history is easier for the mind to fantasize around? Or are there a finite number of souls and does the population explosion mean that we must return to earth more rapidly to make up the numbers?

Notice also that two of the five remembered lives (or two out of six, counting Ray himself) were as females. It is very common for lives of both sexes to be recalled.

own and worked as a boatman in the Millwall docks. One day in April 1879, lonely and depressed, Reuben Stafford jumped into the Thames. His death was relived in eerie detail by Ray Bryant, unaware that the research team had the soldier's death certificate to hand and could compare his story with the truth. Once again, Ray was accurate.

The remarkable normality of this life which spanned fifty-two years, much of it tracked down by Andrew Selby in obscure records, is what makes this case so extraordinary. It is difficult to imagine why anybody would invent – consciously or subconsciously – such a mundane existence. All the information about his life obviously existed in various places, but it is hard to believe that Ray Bryant could have had the opportunity to come across all of it. For

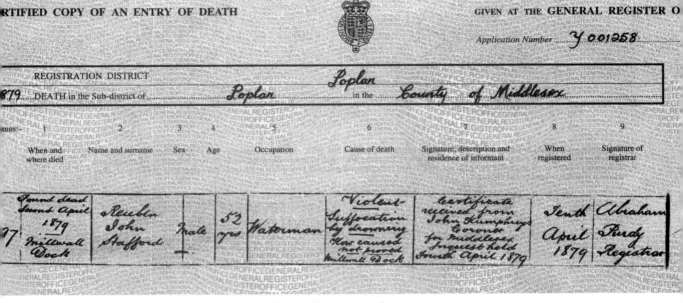

Reuben Stafford's death certificate.

once the very obscurity of the life weighs heavily in favour of it being a genuine case of reincarnation.

WHAT IS GOING ON ?

What is the explanation for these past life memories? Roy Stemman, editor of *Reincarnation International* magazine, says that he has looked into cases for twenty years and 'Ray Bryant's stands out as one of the very best, because there is such a wealth of evidence.'

However, Richard Wiseman, senior lecturer in psychology at the University of Hertfordshire and a cautious investigator of psychic mysteries, warns that things should not be taken for granted.

'There is something called cryptomnesia, which is the idea that when we are young we pick up far more information than we realize – from books, films, other people, etc. This is in our memory, and we have just forgotten about it. But the hypnotist then comes along and suggests we have lived a previous life and all that information comes out.'

Studies have shown that under hypnosis the mind is capable of enhanced memory, so in these circumstances cryptomnesia may well be stimulated. Equally, hypnosis is known to relax inhibitions and give rein to imagination, fantasy and play acting – the basis of all stage hypnosis shows, in which ordinary people are made to do ludicrous things without consciously realizing what they are up to.

Wiseman adds: 'Scientifically speaking, claims of reincarnation are simply very difficult to test. You have to rule out the possibility of a fraud. You have to eliminate the hypnotist feeding information to the subject (unconsciously). The idea that the person has the information in their memory, perhaps from childhood, and has simply forgotten what they know also has to be considered. It is a very messy area. Some of the claims are strong, but even so it is very difficult to know what is going on.'

In Ray Bryant's case, Andrew Selby is persuaded by his own research. 'There is enough evidence to say there is a real phenomenon which is not imagination, not faked. Something is really happening here which needs further investigation.' He also feels certain that 'if Ray was acting we would have caught him out. If it was imagination we would have caught him out. So my belief is that we have a genuine phenomenon here.'

But what? Is the idea that our soul moves from host to host the only possibility? Interestingly, Ray himself is not persuaded that reincarnation is the answer. 'I feel that I have bits of Reuben Stafford in me now. Inevitably he has had an influence on the kind of character that I have become, but I do not think that Ray Bryant was Reuben Stafford.'

But does that mean that part of us survives death? 'Yes,' Ray says. 'I believe that whatever the mind is, part at least survives death. I am not in the least afraid of death, and I used to be very morbid. They can do what they like with the carcass now. That's not me. This is just a case to carry me around in.'

However, he suspects it goes deeper than that. Whilst Ray Bryant cannot decide whether some sort of race memory or genetic inheritance factor might be taking place across the centuries, something is more important than such answers. 'To me the most wonderful thing about all this is not experiencing these memories, as such – although that is quite exciting in itself. But the really marvellous part is that somehow these people's lives continue to go on through my own memories. In the same way, therefore, people I have known who are no longer here are also being remembered somewhere – they are still living on.'

6

SEEING THE LIGHT

Mountain climbing is an activity which captivates thousands of people and yet puzzles many others. Those who have never faced up to their fear of heights, to being cut off from civilization, or to the immensity of our planet find it difficult to understand why anyone should risk their life in this dangerous pursuit, particularly when the reward is nothing more than sheer enjoyment. And those who have pitted their strength and endurance against the world's mountain ranges know how hard it is to explain the intoxicating challenge to non-believers.

Jacqui Greaves, from a small Lancashire town, has years of experience in climbing. On 13 February 1994 she set off with two friends to test herself in Scotland's beautiful Cairngorms Mountains. The intention was a not too strenuous day's climb. But fate was to turn the expedition into a nightmare that could very easily have cost Jacqui her life. Indeed, according to her remarkable story she owes her survival to something utterly inexplicable: in a most unusual combination of near death experience and miracle, Jacqui Greaves believes she was saved from certain death by forces beyond human comprehension.

A PLEASANT DAY'S WALKING

When the little party set off, the weather was magnificent. The bleak, snow-carpeted landscape of Derry Cairngorm, one of Britain's highest peaks, shimmered in the winter sun.

But the Cairngorms are notorious for sudden changes in conditions, switching to the ferocity of an Arctic winter in a matter of moments. This was what rapidly confronted the small expedition as they headed up the

Jacqui Greaves

mountain that day. 'We walked and started ascending,' Jacqui explains, 'but then the weather turned into a white-out and the gales started. It was awful. As we were approaching the summit we decided that we ought to turn back, and we were just thinking about that when I fell.'

The trio were not roped together, as these slopes are not regarded as especially dangerous, particularly in the weather conditions that prevailed when they set out. But now the wind was whipping up the snow reducing visibility to a few inches, and within seconds Jacqui was irretrievably separated from her colleagues. 'I started rolling down the ridge,' she recalls. 'I must have fallen through a cornice. I wasn't scared – just numb. As I rolled and rolled I was just trying to stop myself with my ice-axe. At last I jammed the axe in and stopped, and then the axe flew out of my hands and the crampons flew off my back. And that's where I lay, no axe, no crampons, on the side of a ridge.'

Jacqui had no idea how far she had fallen. There was no chance of catching sight of her fellow walkers – who might indeed have fallen into trouble themselves. Moreover, Jacqui knew that if she tried to move from where she lay there was a real danger that in the swirling snow she could step over the edge of the mountain.

She remembers those first hours on the ledge in the freezing snow. 'I was so cold. Involuntary shivering set in. I could not see. So I got my survival bag out.' This was a huge orange blanket that trapped body heat and helped her to cope with the plunging temperatures which, with the wind chill factor, could reach as low as -30° centigrade. 'I wasn't scared at all. I was just lying there, banging myself, clapping, singing, trying to keep myself warm.'

MISSING

Sergeant Graham Gibb, head of the Braemar Mountain Rescue Unit, knew that bad weather had been forecast for the day. He was hoping that nobody would be deceived by the calm morning sunshine into risking the mountain. But at about 7 p.m. his fears were realized when his telephone rang at home. 'The call came in from Derry Lodge, a mountain rescue point, so our first priority was to get the vehicle out there, get hold of the informant and take him back so that we might get as much information as possible.'

The informant was in fact one of Jacqui's companions. Both he and the third climber, another man, had themselves fallen shortly after Jacqui. The third man had also picked himself up and found his own way off the slopes. The rescue team met him on the way to the lodge.

Sergeant Gibb points out, 'We were reasonably confident that we would find the missing third person quite quickly. The area, we were told, was a small quarry up on the side of Derry Cairngorm. So we were able to concentrate the whole team into there.'

The powerful snowmobile with its caterpillar tracks probed through the night, its pulsing blue lights flickering across the snow. The rescue expedition, including Jacqui's colleagues, marched slowly in front of the machine, holding flares which emitted orange glows and puffs of smoke.

'The team set off in line abreast about 10-15 metres apart,' Sergeant Gibbs recalls. 'We walked into the foot of the cliff. Obviously, if somebody had fallen down we would expect them to be somewhere near the bottom, possibly lying on the snow.' They hoped to find Jacqui very quickly, but failed to do so. Thousands of feet above them Jacqui could see the snaking chain of flares and torches coming nearer, offering hope. She blew the whistle from her survival kit, but it was futile. The rescue party were too far away and the howling wind drowned the sound of her whistling. She watched them disappear into the next valley as her fellow climbers, disorientated by the thickly falling snow, led the rescue party towards the wrong mountain.

INSPIRING LIGHT

'We could not understand why she was not in the quarry,' Graham Gibb recalls. So he sent some of the rescue team higher up the mountain to look at other, smaller, quarries which Jacqui's colleagues might have misidentified in their confusion. 'The team that went up on the top of the mountain encountered quite bad weather,' he continues. 'They decided it would be better for them to stay up in that area rather than come off the mountain and then have to fight their way back up the next day.' This group braved the freezing weather and set up camp, whilst a disappointed Sergeant Gibb led the rest of his men off the slopes and decided to reassess their position the following day.

Jacqui Greaves now faced a sixteen-hour night alone in the snow, yet her spirits were lifted in the most extraordinary fashion. 'All the time I lay there after falling there was a light about 50 to 80 feet above me. It was there all night. It was like a hand torch light, and I thought it was my friends waiting for me to show people the way. It was there until the next morning and then it just seemed to fade.'

Some people might suggest that this could have been the planet Venus, one of the brightest objects in the sky. In very cold weather ice crystals in the atmosphere can create a distortion like a mirage and make it seem spectacularly close. But Jacqui does not think so. 'I don't know what it was,' she says. 'Somebody was telling me to stay there and be safe.'

WHITE-OUT

At dawn the next day Graham Gibb and his team reconsidered their position in relation to where Jacqui's colleagues told them they had been climbing. 'When we looked at the lie of the mountain on the maps we could see that the mountain next to the one they said they were on runs at exactly the same angle. Once you have gone on to the wrong mountain all your compass bearings and map readings would tie in.' He questioned the other two climbers

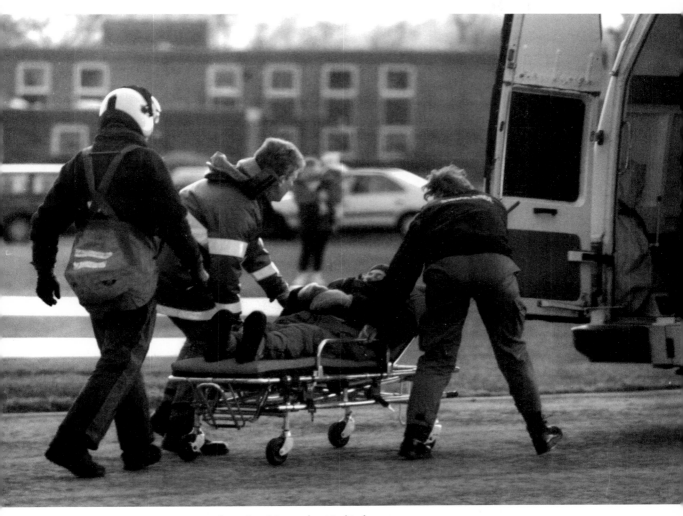

Jacqui arriving at hospital in Inverness.

again, and concluded from what they said that Jacqui was indeed trapped on a different mountain from the one they had been searching the previous night. 'It was at that point that I began to extend the search on to a broader area.' At last they were on the right track, but precious hours had been lost and the sergeant knew that this could make all the difference between life and death.

After surviving the night, Jacqui began to think how to save herself. Taking off her gloves and using her fingers like an ice-axe, she slowly crawled her way down the slope. 'It took me hours and hours,' she grimaces. 'As I got further

Climber tells of her amazing escape from an icy death

MY MIRACLE IN THE SNOW

By JAMES GRYLLS and TONY GALLAGHER

SHE came back from the dead after surviving two nights in the Arctic hell of a Scottish mountain at 38 degrees below zero.

She was finally found by a rescue dog named Solo who bounded up to her. Jacqui recalled last night: 'I said Thank God for that. Then I cried. I thought to myself, it's over.'

Astonishingly, the school secretary from Greater Manchester was suffer-
~~only slight~~ ~~white as she set~~

'I hurtled hundreds of feet down the mountain'

Extracts from the Daily Mail, *February 16, 1994.*

down I started walking and wandering but by then I was exhausted – really exhausted. I think I was getting near to the brink of death.'

It was then that she had some truly remarkable experiences, as she struggled to cope with the white-out that blended the land and the sky into one. 'As I got to the bottom of the slope I was shivering and partly blind. Hypothermia was setting in. Suddenly a barrier dropped in front of me and I stopped.'

It was just like the single barrier found at certain railway level crossings.

Indeed, this is what Jacqui thought that she had come across, and her hopes were immediately raised. 'I thought – this is going to be a railway station and there would be a phone where I could ring for help. But I was still there on the snowy mountains.'

CLOSE TO DEATH

At the point of death about one in ten people have reported bizarre experiences. After being in an accident or desperately ill, they see strange visions. A sense of peace and joy, with freedom from all pain, is even more common. Some people see a bright light, then travel along a tunnel and enter a strange, beautiful land often described as a lovely garden. There may then be a barrier beyond which the person does not travel because they are told to return, or choose to go back to their life.

Jacqui immediately after being found.

In this age of medical miracles more and more people are being revived from conditions which would once have proved fatal, and the incidence of these NDEs (near death experiences) is increasing dramatically. But the question that nobody can answer is whether these are experiences of the final stages of life – hallucinations, for example, produced by chemical changes in the body; oxygen starvation and other body processes are known to induce such visions. On the other hand, these events may be the first glimpses of an existence beyond physical life – one that occurs in some other realm or reality.

Sceptical psychologists such as Dr Sue Blackmore from the University of the West of England in Bristol support the first argument – what is called the 'dying brain hypothesis'. However, other experts cite cases where something veridical is seen by the patient which would have been impossible unless they were really 'out of the body'. This seems to support the idea of survival of death as a real possibility.

Dr Peter Fenwick, neurologist at a leading London hospital and one of the pioneers of NDE research, is coordinating a fascinating series of experiments in which objects are placed in hidden locations at selected hospitals. Invisible from ground level, they could be detected by a patient who was literally floating above their own body.

In fact, as she reached forward and tried to touch the barrier it faded away into nothing. 'There was a hole underneath it,' Jacqui explains. 'Another cornice. I turned around to my right and another barrier dropped – so I leaned out to touch that.' Again it disappeared. Once more, underneath the apparition was a hole in the ice which would have sent the struggling climber to her death. 'Obviously,' she explains, 'somebody was telling me the right way to go.' She turned round and headed back up the slope, where there were no more barriers. Jacqui correctly assumed that this was the safest course to follow.

Hallucinations? Perhaps. But that word hardly disguises the fact that these barriers prevented Jacqui from stepping into certain disaster. Whether they were put there by her mind as a warning or sent by some supernatural intervention is less important than the fact that they saved her life.

THE BLUE LAND

Jacqui struggled onward, unsure where she was headed and with no sense of time. Her mind was freezing like the weather, but she experienced a strange sense of euphoria. 'I just seemed to get a very, very strange feeling,' she reports. 'I left my body and was walking through a beautiful blue land. It was all blue – lovely flowers, trees, bridges. It was wonderful and all the coldness left me.' Jacqui believes that she felt her heart slow down and almost stop before the onset of this exceptional vision. Was she on the verge of death, about to succumb to the trauma of the last twenty-four hours? 'I felt at peace,' she says, remarking that the place reminded her of the scene on a willow pattern plate. 'I seemed to be just drifting.' There was no pain, not even any discomfort. Everything was suddenly peace and pleasure. 'I felt so contented. All my worries had left me. I must have left my body. I was on the way to death.'

But could it have been a hallucination caused by exhaustion and the cold? 'I thought maybe I was dreaming, so maybe it was imagination. But then I just seemed to drift back to the snow. The next minute I was just walking and ploughing through the snow again. I seemed to have a bit more energy, though. It gave me more energy.'

Reinvigorated by her amazing experience, Jacqui pressed on and decided to build a snow hole to protect herself from the cold of the second night that was now fast approaching. Without this shield from the bitter wind she knew that she would enter that blue land for a second time – and not come back again.

Meanwhile, after more frustrating hours searching for Jacqui Greaves Sergeant Gibb was forced to call off the hunt for a second day, even though he knew that it was very unlikely that she could survive another night on the mountain. He said, 'I feared she might have succumbed to the weather. But I knew there was a chance that, if she did have the idea to get out of the wind and protect herself, she could have survived.'

Solo, one of the six Search and Rescue dogs used in the rescue operation. Solo and his handler were the first to spot Jacqui.

Since the odds were growing poorer all the time, for the third day he called in reinforcements: two RAF search teams, the police from the Grampian region, even a specialist dog team trained in seek-and-find operations. More than ninety people would be on the mountain that day, after which all realistic hope would probably have disappeared.

SALVATION

Jacqui knew that if sleep took hold she would never wake up again, so despite her exhaustion, she sang nonsense songs to keep her mind alert.

As on the previous night, there was still a strong sense that she was being watched over by some benevolent force. However, just before dawn, she decided that she would have to climb out of the hole or she would simply give up and die there.

'I climbed out of my snow hole and there were four walls all around me – quite high. So I broke through them.' This was very strange, she insisted, as she knew she had not dug these perfectly constructed, straight walls herself. 'They seemed as though they had been man-made,' she claimed. These towering barriers had held the wind at bay and once again had kept her alive. But where had they come from?

There was something else to ponder, too. The strange glow in the sky was back: 'There was a light that shone between two mountains.' This spectacular softness cast a V-shaped shadow down the slope. 'I quickly put my compass on to that and crawled that way. It was the right way to go. Somebody was showing me the right way to go.'

Soon afterwards a form loomed out of the haze in front of her. 'I suddenly saw a dog and it came up to me and started licking me.' Initially convinced that she was imagining things again, she stared ahead and saw that there were figures following the dog. It was part of the rescue team.

How do we explain Jacqui Greaves' experience? In simple terms, perhaps her courage and resilience saw her to safety. Of course, she also owed her life to the dedication of the rescuers who risked their own welfare in dangerous conditions.

But what of the strange phenomena that surrounded her days on the mountain? Could they all be put down to chance, or was something incredible taking place? Dr Peter Fenwick says her account is more akin to what is called a 'mystical experience' than an NDE. But it does share several features common to that phenomenon. It is also difficult to consider many of the medical theories, such as oxygen starvation, applying to her case – although

Jacqui may have suffered hallucinations due to hypothermia. Some of her account matches stories from other people lost and exhausted in severe weather, which may support that view.

But Jacqui herself says, 'I never felt alone at all. There was always somebody there – a sense of somebody showing me the way to go and what to do. I was sure that without this I would never have got through.'

PART FOUR

GHOSTS AND POLTERGEISTS

The world is full of ghost stories and we love to be thrilled by them.

As stories we can safely remove them from the routine of our lives, convincing ourselves that they have no place beyond the realms of fiction.

Unless you find yourself coming face to face with a phantom.

Certainly, if you live in a grand old house, or ancient castle, you might expect to come upon the odd spectre or two. Tradition almost demands it. But you would hardly imagine that a fishing boat could be possessed, or that an ordinary semi-detached council house would become the scene of one of the best-documented paranormal investigations ever mounted.

Of course, you could take a drive into the country and get away from houses altogether. Then you would be safe. But look out for that hitchhiker standing by the roadside, smiling serenely as you pick her up...

Ghosts come in all shapes and sizes and you find them in the most unexpected places.

7

GHOST SHIP

I magine being out with a small band of fellow fishermen in a trawler, facing the bitter lash of North Sea gales as huge waves crashed against your bows. Such a scene is repeated daily on the seas around Britain. But now think what it would be like if you had to contend with something more than just the known dangers. What if your fishing boat had become possessed by a sinister force?

For the crew of the *Pickering*, sailing out from Bridlington on the North Yorkshire coast, these questions have become more than academic. They have had to confront them in all too frightening reality.

SHIP OF LOST SOULS

The *Pickering* is a 65-foot-long vessel, part of a large fleet that sails from this pretty harbour town. But she has had a tragic history. Jimmy O'Donnell purchased her brand-new from a shipyard in Cork, Ireland, in 1975. The *Family Crest*, as she was then known, was working one December day with another trawler off the coast of County Mayo. A net was cast across the water for them to collect and three of the crew, as usual, made to haul it on board. Unfortunately, they became tangled up in the mesh and were pulled over-board into the freezing waters. Two of the men were rescued, but the third could not be reached and drowned.

As a result of this tragedy, Jimmy O'Donnell gave up fishing and sold his boat. In 1978 she was in Yorkshire, part of Michael Barker's fishing fleet, renamed as the *Pickering* and with her troubled past apparently forgotten. However, events were to suggest otherwise: before long the trawler was at the centre of a series of unexplained incidents.

AGAINST THE LAWS OF PHYSICS

Mick Laws was the skipper of the *Pickering* during the mid-1980s, its early years working off the Yorkshire coast. He well remembers his delight at getting the job. 'At first I was quite excited about it, because it was a bit of a challenge. Nobody had earned any money with the vessel for a long while. As it turned out, it was the worst few months of my life.' The reasons for this growing disenchantment began with sheer frustration. As he explains: 'Everything broke down that possibly could break down. The things that you would not think could break down – they broke down as well.'

However, time was to prove that the problems with the *Pickering* went deeper than a few niggling faults such as you might expect on any large piece of machinery. John Jarvis was mate for Mick Laws and recalls the six months he spent aboard the trawler. 'She was one of the largest boats in the harbour, but she had a way with her that no other boat had. All sorts of things used to go wrong in the wheelhouse – for instance, to the autopilot. Various electrical stuff used to go wrong as well, and there was no answer to it.' As soon as something appeared to be fixed they would set off out to sea, but within minutes further problems would crop up and send them back to port. As John Jarvis pointed out, this unreliability was bad news for the crew. 'There were broken trips all the time. We were not even making our expenses.'

Chris Clark also has good cause to remember the *Pickering*. A senior engineer working for the electronics firm which services the East Coast fishing fleet, he would be sent to investigate any problems that occurred in Bridlington. 'I got called to the *Pickering* many times. Most of the faults were undefined. You couldn't really pin them down. But on one occasion I went to look at the autopilot. Whenever we asked it to go to port it would go to starboard. I changed the wires around to correct this, and everything was OK.'

However, it was to be another short-lived victory. Later that day Mick Laws called Chris out again because the autopilot was proving as useless as ever. Chris was amazed at what he found. 'The polarity going to these two wires had reversed. This is against the laws of physics. In order to put the pilot back to the correct way of operating I had to reverse the wires to what they had originally been. There is no explanation for that at all.'

COLDER THAN ICE

The mechanical problems were not the only reason for disquiet aboard the *Pickering*. Other sinister things were taking place too. 'The boat was very

The Pickering *at anchor in Bridlington.*

eerie,' John Jarvis confirms. 'The cabin was very, very cold. I had to put new heating in, fires, oil stoves – and we still couldn't warm her up. In fact, when we had eight tons of ice in the fish room, it was warmer down there than it was in the cabin.'

When it was decided to take the ship away from its familiar waters and trawl the fishing grounds west of Scotland – renowned for their dangerous seas – the mate decided to call it a day. He refused to sign on board the *Pickering* for another stint. He was not alone in having doubts. Captain Mick Laws recalls some of the other strange episodes that took place. 'One night, just as I got laid down in my bunk, the side of the mattress went down as though somebody was climbing into the bunk above. I actually looked out and said, "Hello", but there was nobody there. I thought nothing of it and I laid down again, but it did exactly the same thing. So I jumped out of my bunk and had a look around the cabin, but there was still nobody there.'

After this frightening scene was repeated for a third time the captain ran to the mess room to confront his crewmates. 'I asked if the lads had been messing about or if any of them had been down there in the cabin.' They had not been. Mick Laws had been quite alone.

However, there were stories about a signature found scratched on to the bunk and the belief was that this may have belonged to the man who had drowned when the ship was in Irish hands. These stories suggested that there might be a link between the weird events that were plaguing the ship and the ghost of her former crew member.

Then, one night at sea, this terrifying prospect was to be remembered by them all. 'We were sitting in the mess room,' the captain explains. 'Barry Mason was on watch. Suddenly the door flew open and it was Barry with this shocked look upon his face. He said he had seen somebody on deck.'

They all scurried up on to the upper deck, with its bright arc lights which twinkled off the water as the ship bobbed up and down. All was calm. There was nobody else on board. But the fisherman was adamant that he had seen a shadowy figure.

A SITUATION VACANT

Visits to the local job centre had become something of a monotonous routine. Whenever the ship proved unseaworthy they could not fish. And if they could not fish they had to find alternative work. They all had families to feed.

In sheer frustration, Mick expressed his disgust to the clerk in the Bridlington office. 'I'm thinking of looking for an exorcist,' he remarked after describing the latest piece of bad luck. It was a throw-away remark borne of exasperation.

The clerk took him seriously and brought over James Trowsdale, the manager. Aside from his work at the job centre, James was a lay reader at a local church. He knew a man who might be able to help.

James says: 'I thought Mick was joking at first – but I had a talk to him and quickly established that there was something very strange going on aboard the boat. Mick was being very serious, so I offered to pass him on to the Reverend Tom Willis, whom I knew from my connections with the church.' The Reverend Willis was an exorcist.

THE EXORCIST

Apart from the usual duties which he performs for his congregation, the Reverend Willis explains, 'I am one of the nine advisers to the Archbishop of York on occult disturbances. We are all parish priests and are called out quite frequently to places and people who seem to have very odd things happening to them. Our job is to have either an exorcism or some ministry of healing to help the situation.'

His task, he says, is to try to bring peace. Such disturbances seem to be on the increase as 'a lot more people have been dabbling in the occult in recent years, and therefore we are getting more calls for help'. He cites the example of a young boy who had become involved with black magic. 'He was having a lot of phenomena happening around him. We tried to get him to come for ministry, but in the end he refused. One day we found him dead in bed, with his arms crossed.' However, the Reverend Willis thankfully can report success more often than failure. 'We recently had a girl brought into church who had been dabbling very heavily in the occult. She renounced what she had done and we anointed and blessed her and commanded any evil to depart. She seemed greatly freed by this, but we had to go back to her house and destroy books of spells and all sorts of paraphernalia connected with what she had been up to.'

When he was informed about the problems on the *Pickering* he talked to various people including Mick Laws and another skipper who had been in charge of the boat. 'It seemed on the surface, straightaway, to be familiar phenomena that were being reported. We had not had a boat before,

Reverend Tom Wills, one of nine advisers on occult disturbances to the Archbishop of York.

CURSED

The Pickering is not the only form of transport to have suffered problems. British Rail faced a similar dilemma in 1981 when a series of disasters began to strike one of its freight locomotives. They even had a telephone call from a woman who said that she had seen the blue engine involved in a crash and could describe the scene vividly. She was able to give the number on the cab of the locomotive – it was 47216. The rail authorities were not inclined to take this story too seriously, although they did check the woman's claim that she had helped the police with her psychic powers. Her claim was seemingly confirmed.

Locomotive 47216 / 47299.

Later that year train spotters noticed something interesting: the diesel had been renumbered. At the time this was quite unusual and tended to occur only when a locomotive had a new engine. Number 47216 had not been altered in this way, but it had been renumbered to 47299.

In late 1983 there was a serious accident when a blue diesel engine carrying oil tankers ran into a passenger coach. The details were very similar to those predicted two years before by the woman with reputed psychic powers – although with one exception. The freight locomotive in the real crash was not numbered 47216. It was 47299.

Whether the renumbering had been carried out in an attempt to cheat fate is not known. British Rail sources suggested that it was just a coincidence. However, the change in number did not affect the curse that seems to have descended upon this engine. Had it been possessed in some way?

A train enthusiast and journalist Paul Screeton, with a special interest in the paranormal, has monitored the chequered career of 47216 (in whatever guise it has since carried) since the 1983 accident. It has had its share of mishaps. Perhaps these, too, were just coincidence – the lot of any working locomotive. However, one wonders if British Rail should not have considered employing the services of the Reverend Tom Willis.

Reverend Willis performing an exorcism.

although we had been to all sorts of buildings. It was really a matter of checking up what people claimed was happening and seeing how many witnesses had experienced this.'

What did his investigation uncover? 'One of the things that the previous skipper had seen was an apparition of a man on the prow of the boat. We felt this rather signified the fact that this was a restless spirit from the past.' After discovering the history of the *Pickering* and learning of the death of the seaman off the coast of Ireland the Reverend Willis concluded: 'We felt that this boat needed prayer and blessing and the commending of the spirit to God.' He next traced the name of the dead sailor and realized that he had probably never had a proper funeral as no body had been recovered. So the minister quickly decided that 'there was a need to exorcise the boat and to pray for the repose of his soul.' A plan was drawn up and Tom Willis set about preparing to exorcise the *Pickering*.

THE CLEANSING OF THE 'PICKERING'

On the day of the exorcism the Reverend Willis made his way along the long stone jetty that leads to the harbour at Bridlington. With him was James Trowsdale, who would act as observer. As they neared their destination a car stopped beside them and its driver asked if they were heading for the *Pickering*. It was the engineer, Chris Clark, on his way yet again to repair equipment on board the vessel, who offered them a lift.

At the trawler Mick Laws welcomed them aboard and thanked the clergyman for coming, although he was unsure what to expect of these strange proceedings. As Chris Clark notes, all those present were 'desperately hoping this would achieve a positive result'.

Opposite *An extract from the* Bridlington Free Press.

Ghostly goings on

Mr Willis, vicar of Holy Trinity Church, exorcised the Bridlington trawler 'Pickering' in 1987 after fishermen refused to work on her, claiming restless spirits had taken control of the vessel.

Supernatural happenings on board the boat meant the steering system suddenly developed a mind of its own, lights started flickering, sudden chills were felt, persistent engine failure occurred and the radar system went haywire at 1.30am every morning.

Mr Willis, an exorcist for more than 20 years, was brought in by the DHSS after investigations were ordered into why the crew of the Pickering were not working.

Dressed in a dark cassock with a purple sash, the Reverend Willis prepared a large golden bowl filled, as he put it, with 'a huge bottle of holy water'. Then he paused and suggested to Mick Laws that it might be a good idea if they put out to sea. This was a practical suggestion, as he had no desire to attract undue attention to what most on-lookers would regard as a bizarre or comical ritual.

Once away from shore, the exorcist made his way across the deck, sprinkling water and praying loudly at the reported cold spots. 'In the name of the Father, Son and Holy Ghost, I command all evil to depart from this vessel.' Then he descended into the bowels of the ship and faced the area around the bunks where Mick Laws had experienced his invisible nocturnal intruder. 'Peace be unto this ship and all who sail in her.' In conclusion he requested all the crew to go on deck and pray. The gathering of fishermen removed their hats and stood with heads bowed as he led them in a moment of contemplation.

PRIDE OF THE FLEET

The day after the exorcism, Tom Willis called Mick Laws to see if there had been any progress. The captain, who took the call on his mobile phone from the bridge of the *Pickering*, was delighted: he reported a completely different atmosphere above and below decks. Everything was running smoothly, and there was no sense of evil or cold spots aboard. 'Reverend', he told the priest, 'I tell you something. You've saved my boat.'

Chris Clark confirms the success. Since the exorcism took place in 1987 the reduction in calls to attend the *Pickering* has been remarkable. Of course, there are still minor faults from time to time but all can easily be put right. Otherwise: 'I am pleased to say that ever since that point there have been no real problems with the vessel.'

Not that this surprises Tom Willis. He says that he was 'very thankful that there did seem to be a real healing', and considers it 'another example of the love of God coming into a disturbed situation and bringing peace to a restless soul.' The *Pickering*'s owner and crew are simply grateful for the peace that has returned to their ship. They agree that it is now a friendly place to work and the trawler has become the pride of the fleet, regularly bringing in the fish that it was designed to catch before something unexplained took hold of its destiny.

8
ECHOES OF THE PAST

The ochre walls of Muncaster Castle are in fine condition, belying its great age. Like many similar buildings dotted across the English landscape, it has a history that is intimately related to the highs and lows of the land that it was built to protect.

This imposing structure stands on the rugged coast of western Cumbria, facing the cold winds that whip in from the Irish Sea and peering out across rolling green hills. It was constructed in 1325 to protect routes south from Carlisle, the city at the frontier with Scotland, along which came both merchants and many an army to guard the borderlands.

Muncaster, however, rarely saw anything that might be described as action. As a result, six centuries later it resembles a sedate country estate more than a battle-scarred fortification. It has not decayed into some long-forgotten monument but is very much a living place – the home to successive generations who care for it and preserve its past with affection.

The manor was in the hands of the Pennington family even before the castle was built, the land having been granted to them by order of King John the century before. Arguably the last 'true Pennington' was the fifth Lord Muncaster, who died in 1917 without direct heirs; the present owner's grandfather, cousin to Lord Muncaster, inherited on condition that his son change his name to Pennington and so maintain the link.

However, despite its seemingly uneventful history, behind the gentle facades of Muncaster Castle something sinister lurks. For its walls resonate with more than just the changing of the times. They may also echo the past in a much more literal sense – by way of something supernatural.

Muncaster Castle, Ravenglass, Cumbria.

AN OPEN-AND-SHUT CASE

Patrick Gordon-Duff-Pennington and his wife Phyllida are the current owners of Muncaster. Patrick has no doubt that strange things happen in the castle. 'I went to open the King's Room one morning and then something pulled the door from the other side.' He is adamant that nobody was in that room. 'The shutters were pulled. So nobody could possibly have done that except some sort of spirit.'

This was by no means the only frightening thing that has occurred in his presence. He has also experienced the ghostly episode most commonly reported in the house. 'I always used to be very cynical about the stories, but every evening after tea in the winter I used to go up to my office between the two high walls above the tea room. And every evening these footsteps followed me, whether it was snowing or raining or fine. It is really quite an uncomfortable feeling.' Even on the morning of his interview for *Strange But*

True? he reported hearing strange clanking sounds coming from one of the empty rooms as he opened the door across the hallway.

Patrick says that his dogs also seem to sense the weird atmosphere. He has often found them sitting by a particular tree in the grounds staring ahead with a curious air. He believes that they can detect the unique ghostly presence in the castle, particularly as this six-hundred-year-old chestnut tree has long been associated with one of the more infamous residents of Muncaster – Tom Fool. Despite the frivolity of his name and the man's reputation as a jester, there are many things about Tom which are less than funny.

PLAYING THE FOOL

Tomfoolery is a familiar phrase today, used to describe actions that are both idiotic and amusing, but once it also had overtones of malice. It has its origin in the legendary story of Tom Skelton, alias Tom Fool, who was the 'last fool of Muncaster' as well as the castle steward in the late sixteenth century. Patrick Gordon-Duff-Pennington explains: 'He was not really a nice man. He used to sit underneath the chestnut tree outside the front door and, if you came and asked him the way back to London, unless he liked the look of you he pointed you down to the quicksands instead of over the ford.'

Whilst this story is widely told, nobody knows if any unwary traveller was ever really lured to his death by Tom, whose forbidding-looking portrait hangs in the house. However, there are indeed very nasty quicksands by the river bank still, and they can prove fatal at low tide.

Researcher and paranormal investigator Jason Braithwaite, who has researched the strange goings-on at Muncaster over a number of years, has delved into Tom Skelton's background and says he belied his 'jester' image and was a sadistic man. 'He was no idiot. In fact he was an intellectual man,' Jason points out. He is also accused in an apocryphal tale of a most heinous crime.

The investigator explains: 'He was supposed to have lured the local carpenter to the Tapestry Room in the castle. This was said to be under the pretence that he was going to meet his love – the Penningtons' daughter. Obviously the carpenter was surprised to see Tom there instead and a short scuffle ensued. This ended up with Tom Fool decapitating the chap with a hammer and chisel.'

According to the legend, which varies somewhat with each retelling, Tom then carried the body outside to be disposed of but proudly showed the head to Sir William Pennington in the expectation that this would meet with his master's approval. While doing so he is also reputed to have cracked a wicked

'Tom Fool's' tree.

joke – which appears to be how 'tomfoolery' came to be associated with ridiculous acts that were also malicious.

TAPESTRY OF FEAR

The Tapestry Room, scene of this supposed crime, seems to be at the centre of many of the frightening phenomena associated with Muncaster. Philip Denham-Cookes, a former curator of the castle, confirms this. 'Muncaster is a friendly place, a homely place. But there were certain rooms which one did not like to go into too often – the Tapestry Room in particular.'

He tells how the rustling sounds of old-fashioned skirts have been reported in the dead of night. Indeed, female visitors seem to be peculiarly upset whenever they go near the Tapestry Room. Denham-Cookes adds: 'I have seen women go to the door and turn around. I have heard them actually say to each other, "I am not going into that room. I don't like it."'

Opposite *The infamous portrait of Tom Skelton, alias Tom Fool, with his last Will and Testament.*

He is even willing to admit that he himself has felt uneasy after locking up at night. 'I always had a feeling in that room that I was being watched.' The late Lord Carlisle once informed Denham-Cookes about a terrifying episode in the same part of the castle. 'I was telling him that I thought it was a most unpleasant room and he told me that he had stayed one night in Muncaster – in the Tapestry Room. Nothing on God's earth would ever persuade him to stay in that room again, because he was woken up in the middle of the night by a baby crying. It went on for about ten minutes. Lord Carlisle was not a man who was easily frightened.'

The former curator has seen something himself, although in another part of the house. 'I came along the corridor, checking the shutters, and I saw this woman come down and turn her back to me. I saw the side of her face as she turned and walked away from me down that corridor. She was wearing a coffee-coloured negligee and she was as solid as you or I. Her hair was done in a bun at the back. I thought some member of the public had got themselves locked in, so I went and checked the door. It was locked on my side, so she had come clean through the door.' At first he thought it was his imagination, but the woman did not disappear in the normal way that visitors do – or, indeed, turn back to him for help to find the way out.'She just sort of faded out,' he reports, describing the manner in which she gave away her ghostly status.

Later he discussed his experience with the castle's owner, at that time Sir William Pennington, who pointed out that his own mother had often worn a coffee-coloured negligee and had her hair tied in a bun. As Philip Denham-Cookes remarked, after that surprising revelation, 'I went and got a stiff whisky. It was the obvious thing to do!'

VOICES IN THE NIGHT

The late Lord Carlisle's anecdote is not the only evidence for something strange occurring in the Tapestry Room. The garden curator Alan Clark, sleeping in the Turquoise Room – next door to the Tapestry Room – one night, reports how the huge wooden doors opened twice on their own when nobody else was anywhere in the vicinity.

Jason Braithwaite has stood in the corridor many times during the tourist season and noticed how women simply walk quickly past the Tapestry Room as if subconsciously made uncomfortable by the mood of distress they sense from within. He has also collected many stories from witnesses on these tours. For example, a woman on a guided walk of the house became separated from the rest of her party as she stared at the menacing portrait of Tom Fool. Then she heard footsteps come up behind her and, without turning round, began to comment on the painting to the other visitor whom she believed had joined her in the corridor. There was no answer. When she did look round she found that she was quite alone. She was so surprised that she checked the nearby open rooms – including the Tapestry Room. But there was nobody else present. Only afterwards did the woman realize that the steps she had heard were walking on stone, whereas the corridor and its

TRAPPED IN TIME

Muncaster Castle is by no means the only old building that is the setting for stories of strange apparitions, noises that echo across empty rooms and mysterious phenomena of spectral origin. In fact, nearly all structures of any antiquity have their legends about ghostly goings-on and even modern houses are not immune.

A popular theory amongst paranormal researchers is that a particularly traumatic or emotional event can somehow imprint itself on to the fabric of the universe and be detected, years or even centuries later, by someone who happens to be in the right place at the right time. The effect is not unlike the replaying of a videotape, which can re-create time and again on your TV screen images and sounds of long-dead people – although these people are restricted to repeating actions that were originally recorded, of course.

It has been theorized that stone rich in quartz crystals might create an electrical field within the building, in effect turning the house into a massive recording medium. Many of the properties involved in what are called time replay apparitions are built out of this kind of rock, such as sandstone or millstone. If a particularly charged event – a murder, for instance, or the desperate longing of a dying person to cling on to the house they knew so well in life – can somehow emit an energy field, this may modulate the natural field within the house and create a time recording that can be 'replayed' at a later date.

Presumably it requires a witness to pick up this signal – or to 'be on the right wavelength', as we perceptively phrase it. Others may only register the residual energy at a lower level, deep in their subconscious, where it creates a feeling of unease. However, every now and then all the right circumstances come together and a replay of the long-gone scene occurs ghost-like before startled eyes.

surroundings were all thickly carpeted. However, the footsteps may have been supernaturally imprinted at a time when the corridor was stone-floored.

James Cartland, a Pennington family friend and archivist, stayed at the castle during the 1980s and became yet another unsuspecting inhabitant of the haunted room. 'I went to bed very late one night and I took some old letters with me to read. I was sitting there snuggled in bed as it was January and jolly chilly. I had not been there very long when this extraordinary feeling came over me. There was a funny noise – like somebody muttering. It became more audible as I listened. I never did discover what the voices were actually saying, but it sounded very much like a child was crying in the distance at the far end of the room.' After a time, as he strained to peer into the darker corners of the dimly lit room, he heard another person enter. 'It was like an adult talking to a child and trying to quieten it down. It really was an extraordinary thing.'

Cartland checked all possible sources of noise, even sticking his head up the chimney to see if the wind was to blame. But it was a calm and frosty night, with no normal sounds to account for the ghostly chatter, and he knew there were no other guests staying in that wing of the castle.

Next morning at breakfast his pallor and sleepless demeanour indicated to the others that something dreadful had happened. When James Cartland explained what he had heard, a fellow guest immediately telephoned her daughter and told her to tell the frightened man what she had experienced the year before.

The young woman is still shocked by what happened to her, despite the passage of nearly ten years. 'I was in bed and I just felt there was something in the room. Then I heard footsteps in the corridor outside. Then the door just opened slightly. I put the light on, but I couldn't sleep. The next night it happened and was far worse. This time I knew that no one else was staying in the castle. Again I heard footsteps outside, but I also started to hear children's voices. It was all right when they were just talking, but then they started chanting or singing. It was horrible.' The girl had been sleeping alone in the Tapestry Room.

Some time after these frightening events, James Cartland made a surprising discovery whilst hunting through old documents in the attics at the castle. 'I was looking at these old plans, and to my amazement discovered that the Tapestry Room was the site of the old nurseries in the middle of the nineteenth century.'

Neither he nor the then teenage girl was aware of any previous stories about children's voices inside the Tapestry Room before they spent their fateful night in the presence of these spectral sounds.

Margaret Susan Elizabeth Pennington,
10 June 1860–8 July 1871
(see page 113).

THE VIGIL

ASSAP – the Association for the Scientific Study of Anomalous Phenomena – was impressed by the way in which the stories about Muncaster all slotted together. So in April 1994 Jason Braithwaite set up a team to spend a night in its most haunted rooms as part of a scientific vigil. Amongst the team with him were fellow ASSAP members Melanie Warren and Ian Topham.

Neither Melanie nor Ian was told where the vigil was to take place, and so had no opportunity to read about the alleged sightings at Muncaster. However, they experienced something strange in the Tapestry Room at 2.45 a.m. Ian reports: 'Slowly a figure walked through the open wooden door and paused. It was three-dimensional but very dark. You could not see any features on it. When it got within a couple of feet of me it sort of vanished.'

A few moments later Melanie Warren entered the room. She had just left the King's Room when 'I saw a shadow going into the Tapestry Room. I assumed it was an investigator and I was just seeing their shadow follow them into the room. I thought I knew where everyone was so that, if an investigator was going in there, perhaps something interesting had happened.'

Melanie, who had followed this shadow into the room, learnt that Ian was the only person present – too far from the door to have reached it in the available time. Melanie reports that Ian looked white with shock as he described what he had just witnessed.

There is a possibility that the figure was another member of the ASSAP team. However, they do not think so, and Melanie Warren has no idea what she saw enter the very room which, although she did not know it at the time, appears to be one of the most haunted in the world.

A SCREAM IN THE DARK

It is clear to paranormal researchers such as those taking part in the vigil that something very strange is going on within the Tapestry Room. Doors opening, shadowy figures appearing, mysterious rustlings being heard are all elements of a classic haunting. But the discovery that this room served as Muncaster's nursery during the last century may be the real key to the biggest mystery of all – the sound of children, crying or singing, that has been heard so often by visitors who spend the night there.

The hunt has been on to identify the possible source of this unusual phantom and a clue has been offered by the present lady of the manor, Phyllida

Muncaster Castle.

The haunted Tapestry Room.

Gordon-Duff-Pennington. She has never encountered anything supernatural herself in the room, but does remember something that may be significant. 'Annie Preston was a lady who lived in the village and died recently at the age of ninety-two. She told me that her grandfather knew Lord Muncaster's daughter.' This girl, named Margaret, was in fact the daughter of the fourth Lord Muncaster, Gamel Augustus, and she died at the age of eleven some hundred years ago. Nobody knows the full circumstances of the child's death, or if she ever slept in the Tapestry Room; although if it

Sacred to the memory of
MARGARET SUSAN ELIZABETH PENNINGTON
only child of
GAMEL AUGUSTUS 4th Baron Muncaster
and his wife
JANE LOUSIA OCTAVIA daughter of
Richard, 2nd Marquis of Westminster

Born June 10th 1860
Died July 8th 1871

Suffer little children to come unto me and forbid them not,
for of such is the kingdom of heaven.
The Lord is my shepherd I shall not want.

Above *The wording of the memorial in Muncaster Church to Margaret.*

was used as the nursery at the time this seems a reasonable supposition. It seems that Annie Preston's grandfather had helped to bury the girl in the church near Muncaster Castle. Phyllida comments: 'He told Annie that this girl had screaming fits before she died. She was obviously ill for some time.'

Do Margaret's deathly agonies linger on in the haunted atmosphere of the Tapestry Room? In the lonely silence of a cold night, are those screams replayed across the centuries to be heard by all who dare sleep within its walls?

9
PHANTOM HITCHHIKER

The fearsome Klein Karoo of South Africa is a desert region some 300 miles east of Cape Town. Route N9 crosses it between Uniondale and Willowmore and seems like any other road in this arid dust-bowl landscape, with its hillocks and scrub bush hiding dangerous gullies. It is a road where care is always essential and fortune is an asset. But on the night of 12 April 1968 both these things deserted a young couple, newly engaged, who were crossing this inhospitable landscape to discuss their wedding plans with the girl's parents.

She was twenty-two-year-old Maria Roux, small, dressed in a black sweater and trousers and wearing a green duffle coat to protect her from the cool night. He was Giel Pretorius, a South African Air Force lieutenant, smiling proudly at his dozing fiancée as he drove the Volkswagen Beetle car.

By the time they passed the Barandas turn-off Maria was deeply asleep. The area is notorious for its high winds. Perhaps that was what caused the little car to leave the road and tumble over the edge.

In the middle of the night Lance Sergeant Pat McDonald heard the phone go at his home and sleepily responded. Calls had to be rerouted this way as the Uniondale station was not considered big enough to be open twenty-four hours a day. He learned that there had been a serious accident near town and explains: 'I went out with the police van and had a constable follow me with the ambulance. On arriving at the scene I found a Volkswagen on its roof off the road at what we call a culvert – a type of bridge with concrete sides. A girl was lying on her back with her head against one embankment.'

The sergeant checked on her condition. 'Her heart was definitely not beating. There was no breathing. Then there was moaning in the car and we assumed there was someone still inside.' It was Giel. He was rushed to Uniondale in the ambulance, but there was nothing that could be done for

Route N9 which crosses the Klein Karoo desert region of South Africa.

Maria. Pat says: 'I got her into the police van and took her straight to the mortuary.' Maria had suffered massive head injuries and had probably never woken up.

SOMETHING TO REPORT

Eight years later, at 8 a.m. on 2 May 1976, Sergeant McDonald received a call from Constable 'Snowy' Potgieter at Uniondale. Pat says: 'When I arrived at the police station in Uniondale, Snowy approached me and told me that something very strange had happened the previous night and did I remember the girl in the accident a few years ago?' The sergeant certainly did remember that terrible accident – eight years earlier, but a tragic scene not easily forgotten.

Snowy seemed stunned by what he had just learned. 'I'll never forget,' says Pat. 'He was actually shocked. He told me: "Read this!"' The constable gave Pat the incident book containing a one-and-a-half page entry which described events from the evening before.

It seems that around 7.30 p.m. a distraught man named Anton Legrange had appeared at the station, where only Constable Potgieter was then on duty. Legrange was evidently desperate to get something off his chest. He had apparently been driving home to Oudtshoorn along route N9 in his new Mercedes Benz car. It was a road he knew well, for he was a truck driver who often drove along it at all hours of the day. On this miserable wet night he had stopped to offer a lift to a young woman who was standing by the road-side looking cold and bereft. The girl was not hitching, but he felt she needed help and looked pale. He suggested he take her the twelve miles or so into Uniondale where she could find some food. In reply there was just a mumble, as there was when he asked for her address.

As they neared their destination Anton turned to talk to the woman once again, but she had vanished. Fearing that she might have fallen out of the rear of his car he retraced his route, scanning the bushes and the roadside as his headlights lit them up. But there was no sign of the girl. It was as if she had never been in his Mercedes.

A Scream in the Night

According to the present station chief at Uniondale, Warrant Officer Mostert, the constable on duty back in 1976 was at first unconvinced by this strange story. 'Potgieter did not believe this man, and thought that he was wasting his time.' However, the driver returned to the police station only minutes after being sent away. This time the man claimed that he had heard a girl scream in the back of his car as he drove past the same spot.

'When Legrange arrived back at the police station,' says Pat, 'he was in a great state of shock. As a matter of fact, he was retching and vomiting. Snowy immediately phoned the district surgeon, who came to give him an injection to calm him down.'

The police officer now agreed to go back on to the road with the terrified motorist and investigate. He followed behind in the police 'bakkie' or van, the high vantage point and probing headlight beams giving the constable a clear view of Legrange at all times. He wanted to make sure that it was

OTHER CASES OF PHANTOM HITCHHIKERS

Stories about hitchhikers who mysteriously vanish are one of the most common ghostly legends in the world. They even pre-date the invention of the automobile, with strangers disappearing from a horse and cart after being given a ride by a helpful passer-by and later identified as someone who once died on that road. It is always difficult to know how trustworthy such stories are, as the motif is now so well known. Indeed it is regarded as a classic urban myth: folklorists write essays about it, assuming it to be largely fictional in nature.

A slightly atypical story is the account offered by actor Telly Savalas, who was best known for his TV role as New York detective Kojak. He tells how, when his car broke down, he was helped by a girl who drove him to safety. Being a gentleman, Savalas insisted on paying her for the petrol she had used. An address was given, but when Savalas arrived to repay his debt the young woman's parents seemed startled. They listened to his story and his description of their daughter, then reported that she could not have given him a lift because she had died some time before.

A nice after-dinner speech, certainly. But how can we know if it is true? Indeed, when many similar tales occur in one area and a legend about a phantom hitchhiker develops, the difficulty becomes greater.

In the South African case the purpose for a fraud seems hard to define, but the story has become so well known that many drivers passing the haunted spot must be aware of the claims, if only subconsciously. This might trigger hallucinations, especially in people driving late at night when the senses are on overload and the mind is tired.

In Britain, the continuous flood of sightings describing a young woman on the road between Chatham and Maidstone in Kent is a good example. They occur in the area of Blue Bell Hill, where in 1965 two young women died in a car accident hours before one of them was due to be married. The frequent sightings of a female hitchhiker who disappears after being given a lift – or of a woman who appears in the road ahead of a car and then vanishes – have spawned one of the biggest ever investigations by the paranormal community.

But we are no nearer discovering the truth. Michael Goss, who has researched and written about the hitchiker legends at Blue Bell Hill and elsewhere, feels that many cases are probably mythical. Yet he admits that some are so strong that the possibility of a real ghost must remain.

Those involving physical evidence, such as the melted cassette adaptor reported by Dawie van Jaarsveld (see page 122) are very rare but consequently become of great importance.

impossible for anyone to open the door of the Mercedes.

As they neared the bridge, the anticipation increased. Then, as Constable Potgieter reported: 'The left-hand back door of the car suddenly opened and closed, and the car veered off the road nearly into the pillar of the bridge.'

Both Legrange and Snowy Potgieter drove quickly back to the police station without looking around. Legrange was told to go home by the back road – a longer journey, but it avoided the culvert. His wife called an hour or so later to confirm that her husband had got home safely, but was in a deep state of shock.

Constable Potgieter locked the station and went home. This would have been completely out of character for a man with a reputation for being level-headed – unless he was seriously concerned. As Warrant Officer Mostert confirms: 'When he saw the door of the car open, I think he believed the story of the ghost.'

WHO'S THAT GIRL?

When Pat discussed these extraordinary events with Constable Potgieter the following morning, several things became clear. First, there was no way the car doors could have opened accidentally: they had been opened by an unseen force. Moreover, Snowy had asked about the fatal accident at the bridge in 1968 for a reason. When Pat gave the constable his description of the dead girl, he was asked to read Anton Legrange's account of what his disappearing hitchhiker looked like. 'Long black

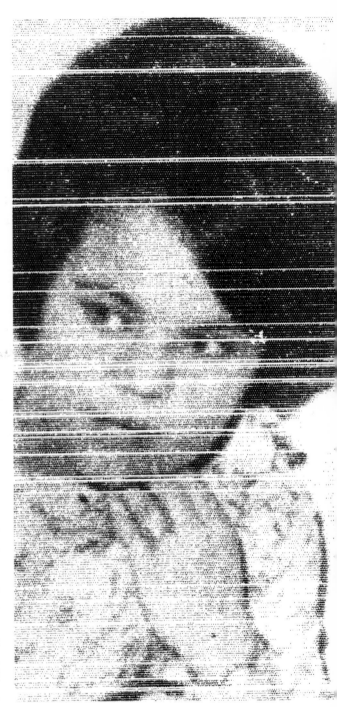

A fax copy of the original photograph of Maria Roux taken two years before her death.

hair, black polo-neck sweater, black slacks – shortish, pretty girl.' It sounded like an exact match with Maria Roux. But it could not be, of course. She had been buried eight years before.

Journalist Janie Meyer investigated this story and was also convinced by Legrange. Contacting Maria's mother, he got hold of a photograph of the girl which had been taken two years before her death. Then a plan was drawn up.

A number of photographs of women not unlike Maria in appearance were taken, along with this picture of her, and all laid before Anton Legrange. Janie describes what happened: 'He immediately pointed out Maria's picture – that was the ghost girl he picked up that night.'

It seems improbable that Legrange had ever met Maria before that night. She had lived in Riversdale, over a hundred miles from his home town. Janie Meyer is certain: 'There was no way that Legrange could have known what she looked like. Definitely not.'

TAKEN FOR A RIDE

In early April 1978 Corporal Dawie van Jaarsveld, doing his national service with the Army, was on his way to see his girlfriend at Louterwater, over 100 miles away. Not familiar with the N9 or its legends, he was passing through the Uniondale area on his motorcycle. To while away the time and keep himself alert Dawie was listening to his personal stereo cassette player, which was beating out the songs of Neil Diamond into his headphones.

He takes up the story. 'When I passed the intersection at Barandas I saw somebody standing there. As I turned off to the right I saw the lady raise her arms. I decided – I can't leave this woman standing there.' So Dawie played Good Samaritan and stopped for the small, pretty, young woman. He asked where she wanted to go and she vaguely indicated a direction. With the tape playing in his ears it was hard to hear her words properly.

Luckily he carried a spare helmet and offered her this, along with a spare earpiece for his tape player. He told her to hold tight and joked that he hoped she liked Neil Diamond. It was all perfectly normal. She held him and he could feel her touch. There was no doubt in the young man's mind that this was a real woman. Until a little further down the road into Uniondale....

Dawie recalls: 'I wasn't going very fast. I felt a twitch on the bike. It felt like somebody was leaving or the back wheel slipping. It was very misty, but I looked around very quickly and I did not see anybody on the back of the bike. I looked in the mirror and got a fright. I saw nobody.' The terrified

THE MAN IN THE ROAD

I have investigated one remarkable case of a phantom hitchhiker for which there is physical evidence. It involved a service engineer named Ken Edwards, who was returning from a union meeting in Manchester late on 17 March 1978. Close to his home at Risley, near Warrington in Cheshire, where there is an atomic energy plant, a strange figure appeared on the roadside. It looked like a man but glowed an eerie white.

Ken pulled his van to a halt as the figure stopped in the deserted road only a few feet ahead of him. The eyes seemed to probe into his body, and he felt very strange and light-headed. Then the figure walked to the far side of the road and passed straight through a ten-foot-high chain-link fence that led into the atomic energy plant. Having done so, it vanished.

Unsurprisingly, Ken was terrified by this experience. When he reached home his wife gave him a large whisky and then drove him to the local police station at Padgate. They launched an immediate investigation, despite the fact that it was now the early hours of the morning. The staff at Risley were also involved because a security breach at the plant could have had major repercussions.

There was no hole in the fence. The figure could not have passed through it in any normal sense. Yet, according to the witness, pass through it he did.

I have spoken with all the key participants, including the investigating police officers, and no explanation was ever found. But perhaps most mysterious of all was that when Ken came to use his van radio transceiver the next day it was useless. Research showed that it had received a tremendous power surge, apparently through the aerial, that had melted the interior and blown circuits - just as Dawie van Jaarsveld claimed had happened with his adaptor.

motorcyclist was sure the girl had fallen off. But then he had another shock. 'I saw the helmet was on the bike. I saw the earphone was still just hanging there.' It was as if nothing of the past few minutes had ever happened.

In Uniondale he stopped at the Petros Cafe. His terror was etched all over his face, as confirmed by the woman owner who later spoke with paranormal investigator Cynthia Hind. The proprietor asked Dawie: 'Have you just seen the ghost girl?' He asked what she was talking about. Not being local, he had never heard the story. She told him about the woman who hitches a lift and then disappears. When he next checked over his bike, he discovered that there was a problem with the adaptor that ran from the battery and powered his cassette player. Dawie says: 'The whole adaptor had melted down. I could not use it again and just chucked it away.' Nor would his girlfriend ever wear the helmet that had been bought for her use but had been briefly borrowed by the girl who never was.

NOT AT PEACE

Dawie van Jaarsveld's description of the young woman is chillingly familiar. 'She was wearing dark clothes, jeans, a dark jacket ... she was not very tall.' Again this seems to be very much like Maria Roux.

The Army man rode on to his girlfriend's home and did not make any attempt to sell the story to the press or to talk about it. Janie Meyer learned about the case from the woman at the Petros Cafe and it was a tough job tracking down Dawie van Jaarsveld, but he succeeded. Of their eventual meeting, Janie says: 'I definitely believed him. He had no motive. He definitely assured me that he had never heard of this girl before.'

By now there had been several reports of this vanishing woman, of which the encounters of Legrange and van Jaarsveld are the most graphic. It was becoming apparent to local people that all the sightings seemed to occur in March or April, often late on wet nights and just after Easter, around the same time that the tragic road accident had occurred at the culvert. Furthermore, the witnesses were always young men driving on their own.

Was this the ghost of Maria Roux, still trying to find her way home? Had she died so suddenly in her sleep that she did not even realize that she was dead? Was her restless spirit searching for peace? Whatever the truth, the legend of the ghost girl was firmly in place.

THE GHOST GIRL RETURNS

Sightings of the mysterious ghost girl on the N9 near Uniondale continue to be reported.

In April 1980 André Coetzee was waiting for a friend who was riding his motorcycle from Johannesburg. Petrol restrictions were in force which meant that fuel could not be purchased at night, so André was waiting with a supply to top up his friend's bike and enable him to conclude his long journey.

André Coetzee who encountered the ghost girl in April 1980.

His friend did not show up, but while André was in the area on his own motorcycle something terrifying occurred. He says: 'As I reached the Barandas turn-off all of a sudden I felt these hands around my waist. As I looked down – they were more or less like human hands. And I saw her legs as well. I realized that this was the ghost woman of Uniondale. Then I started accelerating – about 150 or 160 kph. She gave me three whacks against my helmet and then just disappeared.'

André was a local and he knew the stories well, though he claims not to have believed in them and had no idea of what this phantom figure was supposed to look like. However, when he was later able to give his account to the police it was found to be yet another description of a woman just like Maria Roux.

So shaken was he by this experience that André could not ride home, and wanted to stay where there were lights and people. In the cafe in Uniondale he met a man who offered him a bed for the night, but as they were talking something amazing happened outside. There was nobody near his motorcycle. He had the only set of keys in his hand, but as André says, 'We heard the motorbike start... the headlights went on, went off again and the bike shut down.'

Janie Meyer explains that reports still come in of odd things on the road and vague stories from people who claim to have confronted the ghost girl. But none have surpassed these three cases – Legrange, van Jaarsveld and Coetzee.

So sure is he that the girl is out there that he has not been content to sit and wait for the stories to come in. 'I have been out there on three occasions at Easter already, looking for her. I took my camera. I thought she might decide to get in if I was there – a guy alone in a motor car. But she didn't.'

But he will keep on trying. And what if he succeeds and does pick up the ghostly hitchhiker?

Meyer says wistfully: 'I will try and take her back to where her parents used to live.'

10

THE ENFIELD POLTERGEIST

Enfield, north London, in the summer of 1977 would be most people's image of pleasant suburban life. It would certainly be one of the last places you might expect to find the supernatural at work. However, that can be just where strange phenomena are at their most insidious.

The Hodgeson family lived, as they had done for many years, in a typical unassuming semi-detached home. Peggy Hodgeson was struggling to bring up her young family on her own after the break-up of her marriage a couple of years before. 'There was a lot of stress in the house at the time – a lot of upset,' Peggy said, adding that she felt sure the children – particularly her two daughters, eleven-year-old Janet and thirteen-year-old Margaret – had picked up on this. However, many families are similarly troubled in modern society without suffering the trauma that the Hodgesons were about to face.

Out of nowhere, their ordinary lives were struck by a force that none of them could understand. Even to this day, with the anguish just a memory, they look back at eighteen months of living hell and wonder what they did to deserve it. They had found themselves, for a time, at the mercy of one of the best-documented and best-authenticated poltergeist outbreaks in paranormal research history.

'I cannot forget it,' Margaret, now thirty-one, admits. 'I can put it out of my mind now – but only now. Through most of my early and middle twenties I could not even talk about it. I'd be in tears all the time.' This response is clearly at odds with those critics who once accused the two girls of perpetrating a hoax. For both Margaret and the rest of the family this complex affair was much worse than a childish game that got way out of hand.

KIDS WILL BE KIDS?

Peggy remembers that first sultry night, just after the August bank holiday. 'It was late one evening and the children were in bed. I had gone up as well and after a while I heard this shuffling noise. I kept saying, "Break it up in there!" to the children, thinking they were making the noise. But they kept saying, "It's not me, it's not me!"' In the end, frustrated by their protests, Peggy went to check and realized that both the girls and her two young sons were not misbehaving, just as they had insisted. They seemed as mystified as she was. In fact, the girls claimed, with evident fear, that a chest of drawers had suddenly jumped across their room on its own. They were adamant that this was not their imagination, and Margaret, who was studying for exams, told her mother she was not sleeping in that room tonight.

Reluctantly, Peggy went to disturb the Nottinghams next door. Three men from that household came to investigate the sounds, which, they logically suggested might have been caused by mice. The men looked everywhere, but found nothing. Then as they came downstairs there was a knocking sound going down the side wall where the stairs were. Vic Nottingham, believing now that burglars were trying to get into the house, rushed outside to try to find the culprit. But there was nobody in sight.

Peggy finally made up her mind to call the police. When WPC Caroline Heeps arrived, with a male colleague, they made a quick search of all the rooms – even though they seemed doubtful of finding anything. 'Have you looked in the loft?' the policewoman finally asked, still suspecting it was a false alarm.

Then, just as WPC Heeps was advising Peggy not to be concerned, more scraping and shuffling began. All eyes turned across the living room towards the source of this new sound, and the whole group, including the Nottinghams and the two police officers, saw a small wooden chair wobble, then slide several feet across the floor as if pulled by some unseen force. Now they knew the truth. These events had no rational explanation.

SLEEPLESS IN SUBURBIA

Much of the early activity seemed to focus on Janet. But her older sister Margaret witnessed a great deal, and all the family were soon directly ensnared. Margaret recalls: 'None of us could really believe what we were seeing – the knocking and things that started to fly about. I said, "I'm frightened", and Janet was crying. My brother was in a turmoil. My mum was shaking.' All they could do was hope that it would go away, as nobody seemed either willing, or able, to do a thing to help them. Margaret explains: 'The fear that went through you – with anyone older it could bring on a heart attack. It was that frightening.'

Peggy was even more desperate. 'I was trying to keep calm because of the children. I did not want to frighten them any more than they were already. But it was very difficult.' The five of them took blankets and pillows and settled downstairs. They spent many nights like that in the weeks to come, afraid to sleep in their own rooms upstairs.

SOMEBODY HELP US

Peggy Hodgeson's desperate pleas for help were answered; although not in a way that she immediately understood.

Graham Morris was a photographer working for the *Daily Mirror*. He remembers how his paper was to take that first step on the road to salvation for the Hodgeson family. 'I was doing a late shift and the phone rang about half ten and the news desk answered it. I remember them saying, "Yes, okay lady, phone back when the pubs are shut," and putting the phone down. We used to get a lot of cranks phoning up.' But this was no crank call. It was the Hodgesons' neighbours asking the paper to come and try to help the beleaguered family. Thankfully, they did call back after the pubs were shut – although none of them had been near one, of course! This time the urgency in the Nottinghams' voices was all too apparent to the news desk.

So Graham became part of an investigating team on the strangest assignment of his career. He then recalls arriving at the Nottinghams' home and then entering the 'haunted house' next door for the first time. 'They were genuinely upset. I mean, they were frightened. It was quite amusing, really – we were all trying not to be the first one through the door.'

Once inside they all stood in a ring and called out into the darkness. Nothing happened. 'Then suddenly all these bits and pieces started flying around. Small household objects were whizzing through the air on their own!' Graham adds: 'I was fairly sceptical and watching the children. They did not appear to be throwing anything. Their arms were not moving. I was over in one corner of the room to get the widest angle for my photography and I got hit on the forehead by a Lego brick. I saw it coming for the last few inches, but not enough to duck out of the way.'

A LENGTHY INVESTIGATION

This evidence persuaded the media to take on the story. The *Daily Mirror* decided to subject the case to a long-term study, for which Graham and his photographic expertise would be essential. Two reporters and two photographers were sent to Enfield.

On 30 August 1977 the *Daily Mirror* published its report. It was read by Maurice Grosse, a man with a lifetime interest in the paranormal, but who had had no direct involvement in the field until a recent family tragedy. 'I had only joined the Society for Psychical Research – the SPR – about a year before. I had joined because, unfortunately, my youngest daughter was killed in a motorcycle accident and some very extraordinary things happened just before and after she died. Because of my interest in the paranormal I thought I must take it very seriously.'

The SPR, formed over a century ago by some of the leading intellectuals of the age, is the oldest and best-respected scientific research group in the world. Its members are involved with a wide range of spontaneous paranormal activity, and cases of ghosts and poltergeists have been two of their most active areas of work. Secretary Eleanor O'Keefe knew that Maurice had asked to be informed if and when the SPR needed someone to investigate a poltergeist outbreak in his area. His chance came when the *Daily Mirror*, frustrated by five days in the Enfield house without much idea what to do, and unable to advise the Hodgesons on how to cope with the nightmare, asked the SPR for urgent help.

'I was expecting to go on a case that was going to last about three weeks,' Maurice recalls. 'Because that's what poltergeist cases are usually like. Little did I know that I was going to be on this one for six months, literally day and night, and I was on the case for over eighteen months altogether.' For the would-be ghostbuster his greatest test was about to come at the very start of his career in the supernatural.

FIRST IMPRESSIONS

When Maurice Grosse first entered the house, about a week after the outbreak began, he was fortunate in that many other people had been there before him. They included assorted family members and neighbours, local and national reporters, a priest and the police. So there was plenty of independent corroboration that strange things were taking place.' The atmosphere when I got there was absolutely chaotic,' he recalls. 'Everybody was in a terrible state. Nobody knew what was going on, and this was one of

POLTERGEISTS

Poltergeist is a German word which translates into English as 'rattling ghost' or 'noisy spirit'. There have been tens of thousands of cases recorded from all over the world, and outbreaks have struck everywhere from primitive tribes in the jungle to high-rise apartment blocks in major cities.

Typical phenomena reported include objects moving apparently of their own accord, things materializing and dematerializing (seemingly out of nowhere), pools of water or other liquid suddenly forming inside houses, and strange lights and noises plaguing rooms. More ghostly attributes, such as the sighting of apparitions, are less common.

Theories on the cause of this bizarre activity vary. Many sceptics put it down to fraud, although the sheer scale and long-term history of the phenomenon seems to argue against this except in a small number of cases. It has long been noted that many poltergeist outbreaks centre on young people, often girls, around the age of puberty – in other words, between the ages of ten and sixteen. This has led to speculation that the physical and emotional turmoil through which they are going is somehow externalized in a completely unconscious way as a sort of 'psychic temper tantrum'. Research into activity within the right brain hemisphere is suggesting a possible source for such energy. At the other extreme is the idea that poltergeists are really the product of deceased humans, or ghosts, trapped in the earthly realm and taking out their frustrations or simply seeking attention.

LIGHT BULBS TURNED GREEN, EGGS FLEW OUT OF THEIR BOXES, PICTURES FELL OFF THE WALL ... IT ALL HAPPENED TO AN ORDINARY FAMILY IN NORTH LONDON.

The house of strange happenings

By GEORGE FALLOWS and DOUGLAS BENCE

A FAMILY is living in fear of strange goings-on that are driving them from their home.

For two weeks, they have been terrorised by objects inexplicably shooting through the air, or furniture moving for no apparent reason. Two clergymen have blessed the house but the happenings have the good things about the case as far as I was concerned. I realized it must be genuine.'

He spent the first couple of days observing the reactions of the family. With four children that was an important step, as it would be hard to keep track of them at all times. 'I watched them like a hawk. I was literally following them around, and I realized that nobody was doing anything. I knew then that the case was real. I brought in my tape recorders and had them running all the time. Guy Lyon Playfair, another researcher, had by then come on to the scene. We discussed it and decided to get the family involved in investigating their own phenomena.'

Maurice explains that he and Guy did not want to appear as experts who knew everything and could sort out the mess with ease. They knew it was not going to be as simple as that.

'I explained to Mrs Hodgeson and the children, as best I could, what poltergeist phenomena were all about. Janet made me laugh because she did not even know what the word was. She used to call it a polka-dice. It was quite evident that the children and the mother knew nothing about the phenomenon whatsoever – which was important, because that meant they could not be imitating it.'

HOT MARBLES

Maurice Grosse had his first direct evidence of what he was up against only a couple of days after starting his investigation, when he was attacked by flying objects in the house. 'A marble shot across the room and hit me. I thought: my God, nobody has thrown that, because there was nobody in a position to throw it. Now if you drop a marble on the floor it bounces. These marbles used to hit the floor and stop dead, and when you touched them they were hot. This is typical of psychokinetic phenomena such as have been reported in other poltergeist cases. So the evidence was beginning to build up even from the first few days.' He says that the marbles were not just warm, as if they had been held in someone's hand, but hot as if they had come straight out of an oven.

Luckily, he had an understanding wife and had just sold one of his inventions for a considerable sum of money, so he had the luxury of being able to spend as much time with the Hodgeson family as was necessary. Maurice soon became virtually a full-time resident, often staying all night or arriving before breakfast. But the pressure took its toll. 'One time I was quite ill,' he points out. 'I had to stay away for about ten days, because it really got on top of me.' But most of the time he was like one of the family. 'I found the children delightful. I think they treated me as a bit of a father figure. But that was no bad thing.'

UP, UP AND AWAY

As things progressed, Maurice and Guy brought in other suitably qualified people to lend their expertise. They included David Robertson, a physics researcher at Birkbeck College, London University.

One night the girls were complaining that objects like their slippers were

Janet, in one of her trance-like states, with Maurice Grosse.

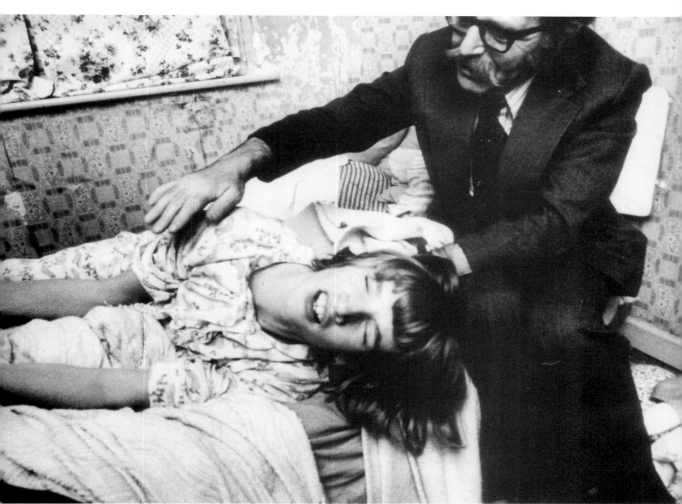

*An apparently unconscious Janet, lying on top of a radiogram,
is discovered by her uncle, John Burcombe.*

being tugged off and cast around the room. David was unable to tell if they
were kicking them off. So, after initially handing back the objects, he began
to pile them up in the centre of the room until, eventually, most of the easily
movable and accessible objects had ended up there. His strategy was to try to
coax the poltergeist into moving larger, heavy objects instead.

Then, as if in response, something came at him from the fishtank above
Janet's head. 'It was a large glass plate like an ashtray, and it flew across the
room and struck me quite a blow on the side of the head. So I concluded that
I had observed something paranormal and that it probably wasn't wise to
carry on with that line of experimentation.'

This was by no means the heaviest item to be tossed around. On one occasion the very heavy sofa turned upside down. Tables and chairs did that frequently, sometimes immediately the door was closed after the last person had left the room.

But the most frightening episodes of all concerned the trance-like states that Janet fell into. Maurice Grosse was quite concerned during these attacks. 'She was so violent that she used to rush across the room and smash her head on the wall. We used to have to physically restrain her.'

One night, around midnight, Janet was so bad they had to call a doctor. He injected her with enough Valium to knock out an adult, let alone a child. She was then settled into bed. All the other children had long been asleep. Maurice was downstairs with Peggy's brother John Burcombe. 'Forty minutes later there was an enormous explosion,' Maurice recalls. 'I thought the roof had blown off the house. We rushed upstairs. John got there first, swung the door open, rushed into the room and looked at the bed. Janet had gone!'

Thankfully, she had not really vanished. A photograph taken automatically at that moment of discovery by a camera set up by Graham Morris depicts her on the far side of the bedroom, still deeply unconscious, perched on top of a large radiogram that was itself resting on a chest of drawers (see opposite).

COME FLY WITH ME

Janet was found twice more that night on top of the radiogram. How she got there while fast asleep remains a mystery. Maurice Grosse says: 'It was absolutely incredible – I mean just inexplicable.' John Burcombe, whose shocked expression on finding Janet was recorded on film, admits, 'That was scary.'

The idea that Janet (and, to a lesser degree, Margaret) might be flying or levitating like this was a firm possibility, especially after another experience recalled by John. 'I was just about to go, standing at the living room door, and Janet was lying on the couch opposite asleep. I just said to Peggy, "I'm off," and suddenly Janet started to move. I looked and she was coming up, dead straight like that, floating into the air. Suddenly she came at me in a rush. She ended up on the floor. My glasses were knocked off and I was lying on the floor holding my face, thinking: they are never going to believe this at the casualty department.' Thankfully, John was unhurt and Janet was still fast asleep. But had she really levitated? Both Peggy Hodgeson and Margaret confirm that they saw this actually happen.

Janet, in flight, watched by her mother and sister.

On another occasion John watched both girls bouncing up into the air about 6 feet from their beds, flat on their backs but behaving as if on a trampoline. Physicist, David Robertson decided to test this incredible claim. He stood in the hall with the bedroom door open to let him peer inside – the phenomenon would not happen if he stayed in the room. Janet described from the bedroom how she was being lifted up and was turning somersaults. So, as the scientist explains, 'I gave her a pencil to write her name up on the ceiling. She managed to put some scribbling up there, but not to write very clearly. Then, about halfway through the session, the bed slammed up against the door with a tremendous crash.' The girl now reported from behind the sealed-off door that a cushion had been sucked through the closed window, where it had disappeared as if by magic. Now she was 'being lifted up near the windows and the curtains were blowing around'.

SEEING IS BELIEVING

These stories sound particularly amazing, and any cautious analyst is bound to be suspicious since the researcher was not able to see what was taking place. However, down in the street below there were people who claim to have witnessed this extraordinary scene.

Delivery man John Rainbow says that he looked up at the bedroom and 'the curtains were billowing inwards and a young girl seemed to be floating around in the room, like she was in a bubble. I couldn't believe what I was seeing.' Hazel Short was a lollipop lady, looking after a school crossing point near the house that day. She noticed with surprise a red cushion perched on the slates of the roof. She is adamant that it was not there a little while earlier, as it was easy to spot from where she waited for her next turn of duty. She confirms that the window was closed. However, she too saw that the curtains were billowing as if in a breeze.

Later David Robertson retrieved the cushion, but says Janet was too small to have put it on to the roof, given the layout of the bedroom and the lip that surrounded the tiles above the window. Hazel also saw Janet. She reports that the girl was 'floating, or levitating, up and down – just going up and down in front of the window flat on her back. I thought she was putting it on, I must admit, because I found out afterwards that her bed was situated under the window. So I went home, lay on my own bed and tried to lift myself up horizontally. You could not do it. Not even halfway up the window frame. No way.'

Graham Morris attempted to provide photographic evidence of these levitations. Sadly, video cameras were not practical for psychic research in 1977, so all he could do was set up still cameras in the closed bedroom that would be triggered by movement or noise and would then take a run of pictures in quick succession. He managed to get a sequence of images that show the girls in mid-flight and then having crashed on to the floor out of bed. But are they flying or jumping? And what is his opinion of these famous shots?

Graham is admirably frank in reply. 'Well, the pictures were genuine. What the reason was behind the girls coming out of bed, I don't know. I mean, people talk about levitation, but I find that very hard to believe. It was quite honestly just a few pictures of a girl coming out of her bed – leaping, jumping, getting out – whatever.'

MATTERS ARISING

This honest comment about the levitation phenomenon is only reasonable from a cautious observer who was not present in the room. But what of the views of the people who were there?

Peggy Hodgeson describes how she went into the bedroom on another occasion when levitation occurred (unfilmed). She says she watched it with her own eyes. 'I sat on the end of one of the girls' beds and I saw her – she dropped on the floor and then got back into bed. Then the other one was coming out. They seemed to rise up as though they were being lifted and tossed on the floor.' She is sure they were not jumping – such an act would give rise to 'a different reaction' from the girls. 'No,' she says, 'They were being lifted. You could see that.' Had she tried to hold her daughters down? 'No,' she admits, 'I was too scared.'

Margaret can offer a first-hand perspective on these alarming episodes. 'It wasn't really like someone touching me. It was more like a pressure. The atmosphere of the room would go cold and you would feel really chilly and want to put on jumpers. I always felt the pressure behind me, but I could never feel anything in front. I just felt there was something behind me – watching me – and then something would happen.'

THE VOICE

After several months of activity – sometimes infrequent, at other times constantly throughout the day – Peggy Hodgeson was getting exasperated. 'I did feel at one time that we had got it for life. I thought: this is worse than the war. At least the war ended.'

So Maurice Grosse changed tactics and tried to communicate with the force. Using the old ploy used in seances, he asked questions and suggested one knock for yes, two for no – and a contact of sorts was established. The message came through that the source of the problem was a man who had died in the house several years earlier. Maurice was unsure how to take this new 'evidence'.

Then, on 10 December 1977, a phenomenon occurred that was remarkable even by the standards of those that had already been experienced in this house. 'I was sitting in the lounge with Mrs Hodgeson and the children,' Maurice Grosse recalls. 'They were exhausted and had been to sleep very late. We were just talking casually when suddenly a dog barked in the room.' The only odd thing about such a mundane event is that there was no dog in the house. Later, Maurice and Guy Lyon Playfair concluded that, if the poltergeist could make barking sounds, then perhaps it could also speak. That night, with many witnesses and his tape recorders switched on, Maurice decided to take the initiative. He would challenge the voice to talk!

After a while it uttered the word 'Maurice' in a husky voice. The researcher says: 'Even I was taken aback. It really was quite a shock to hear it. It was a deep, gruff male voice talking in a staccato manner.' At first the voice insisted that the researchers must leave Janet and Margaret alone in the room, or else it would not speak. But, after a while the investigators were able to remain as the voice continued to talk. 'I realized that the voice was coming from Janet,' Maurice Grosse notes. 'But she denied this, saying that it was coming from behind her instead.' It was astonishing.

How did Maurice feel when this amazing new twist unfolded? He says: 'I can only use one word – wonderment. I was actually there and appeared to be talking to somebody who said he had died fifteen years ago.'

TRACKING THE SOURCE

Over a year of detailed communications with the voice were to be recorded. Most of the time it seemed to emerge from Janet, but Margaret, Peggy and one of the boys were also later 'used' in this way. The sound is very similar to that which people adopt when they lose their voice, and comes from the false vocal cords. A technique used by ventriloquists is relatively easy to do for a short time, but serious throat trouble normally results if it is practised at any length. Yet this voice was sometimes speaking for hours on end, day after day – so it was very unlikely to have been a piece of conscious trickery performed by Janet or the others.

John Burcombe was present during many of these sessions. He says: 'I never at any time saw Janet's lips move, but many times I had conversations with this voice. The language was very gutterish. It was crude – to be polite.' When he asked the force behind the voice to show itself it said, 'I can't – I'm dead.' When John joked about what dead people were like, the voice said 'Go away you four-eyed git!'

Margaret describes what it felt like when this bizarre voice spoke through her. 'It felt like something behind me talking like that which was following me around.' Even years later the voice would occasionally emerge, she adds, when she was sitting alone in the house.

The researchers tried all sorts of methods to investigate this mystery. They sealed the girl's mouth shut with a piece of tape. Still the voice came out.

They attached microphones to the front and rear of the throat and established that the voice was emerging mostly from the back of the throat. Finally, they borrowed a machine called a laryngograph from London University. It monitored the pitch at which the vocal cords operated and proved that the origin of the voice was as suspected – the false vocal folds above the larynx.

CHILD'S PLAY

By the autumn of 1978 the events in Enfield had begun to fade. Soon Maurice Grosse was able to return to his normal life, with the eternal thanks of the Hodgeson family who feel he saved their sanity. Janet spent time in the Maudsley Hospital, a top psychiatric unit, after which she was given a clean bill of health. Now married with a family she runs a nursery and prefers to forget all about the poltergeist. Margaret still lives with her mother in the same house. They have thought of moving once or twice, but two families rejected the property when they heard about the ghost. However, the Hodgesons seem content to live there now that things have died away. Margaret believes that once they overcame their fear of the poltergeist it lost its hold over the family.

Maurice Grosse says this is how poltergeist cases tend to go – eighteen months is quite a lengthy spell for such a case. But he has had critics, some of whom are fellow researchers. They suggest he was either taken in or was encouraging the children's play-acting. But Maurice responds philosophically, pointing out that they did, naturally, play the odd trick or two. What children in such a position would not have done? But he thinks that he was able to spot such occasions quite readily.

'Of course, I was suspicious of the children from the word go,' Maurice admits. 'But I had to look at the whole scene. If the children are capable of doing tricks, that's one thing, but when you get a whole lot of people who have been in the house and they are all in a state of chaos I thought to myself: how can it be the children? Because in the end if it was the children we had the world's best conjurer and we had the world's best ventriloquist – all from a little eleven-year-old girl. This was, of course, ridiculous.'

MY NAME IS BILL

So who was the alleged communicator behind the voice? He had given his name as Bill and claimed to have died in the house fifteen years earlier, when

Printed by authority of the Registrar General.]

CERTIFIED COPY of an ENTRY OF DEATH
Pursuant to the Births and Deaths Registration Act 1953

HC 346015

D. C
S.R

Registration District   Edmonton

1963. Death in the Sub-district of Enfield   in the County of Middlesex

Columns:—	1	2	3	4	5	6	7	8	9
No.	When and where died	Name and surname	Sex	Age	Occupation	Cause of death	Signature, description, and residence of informant	When registered	Signature of registrar
	Twentieth June 1963 Enfield	William Charles Louis WILKINS	Male	61 years	Stores Foreman (retired)	1a Coronary Thrombosis Certified by HDG Barnes MRCS	E.M.Wilkins Widow of deceased In attendance Enfield	Twenty first June 1963	E.Bonser Registrar.

Certified to be a true copy of an entry in a register in my custody.

.... Superintendent Registrar.

CAUTION:—It is an offence to falsify a certificate or to make or knowingly use a false certificate or a copy of a false certificate intending it to be accepted as genuine to the prejudice of any person, or to possess a certificate knowing it to be false without lawful authority.

6.6.95 Date.

A copy of the death certificate for William Wilkins (with address deleted to protect confidentiality of family). Has the Enfield poltergeist finally been identified?

he had a haemorrhage, in a chair, downstairs. Perhaps the most dramatic twist came a few years later when Guy Lyon Playfair received a letter from a man who told him that his uncle had died in the house some time before the Hodgesons moved in. During research for the programme his death certificate was traced. It proves that he did indeed die there in 1963, nearly fifteen years before the poltergeist activity began. His name was William Wilkins – but of course everyone would have known him as Bill.

PART FIVE

MYSTERIES OF TIME

Physicist Albert Einstein defined time as 'what clocks measure'. Time passes, we experience its flow and our instruments record it – according to rules that we lay down. Indeed some scientists wonder if we have invented time as a means of disguising the ineffable nature of the universe.

Even if time is just an illusion, we can still feel its sting.

Thoughts, deeds and retribution cross the centuries. The power of the curse survives today despite a decline in superstitious beliefs. Some say it weaves spells through belief in its potency – but what of curses where the effects are real yet the victim is unaware they have transgressed a hidden power?

There are even those who say they have travelled in time. Such timeslips are an accepted part of paranormal research. They are rare, but according to apparently trustworthy witnesses, they do happen. In a timeslip, the witness enters another age and stays there, perhaps briefly, before returning home.

Slips of short duration are remarkable in themselves. But what if there are four of you, sliding backwards through decades, not just momentarily, but living and sleeping in the past?

Is time more than 'what clocks measure' after all?

11
FOREVER CURSED

The Scottish Highlands are wild and magnificent, with dramatic scenery that people travel thousands of miles to experience. Off the coast are numerous islands, some large, some small, set against the majestic backdrop of the restless Atlantic. Many of these rocky outcrops are accessible only by air or infrequent ferry services. They become time capsules, trapping their communities in a way of life that changes far more slowly than elsewhere.

Since people first inhabited the northernmost parts of Scotland a special bond has linked these places. Off-islanders, although welcomed, are always regarded as outsiders and find it difficult to adjust to the centuries-old traditions which permeate the lives of the local people. This is the way of things in South Uist, a remote, picturesque island of the Outer Hebrides chain. The moss-encrusted, pale grey rock was first inhabited around 3000 BC. Today the island's stone-built houses and chapels seem little different from how they must have been a thousand years ago.

Ruled over by the Clanranald clan for many centuries, most of the families here can trace their ancestors back through numerous generations and in many cases link themselves directly to the clan. This makes anything connected with the Clanranald history an integral part of island life. If a Clanranald is wronged, the island responds.

It is not surprising that this place, fuelled by such unfathomable highland spirit, maintains a rich history of legend and superstition. This is much more a part of day-to-day life than would be true in the cities of Glasgow and Edinburgh. These places are less than 200 miles south-west of Uist, but in many respects they are a universe away.

THE CLANRANALD CURSE

'There's a strong possibility that there is some strangeness attached.' So says Neil MacMillan, one of the islanders, talking about the legends surrounding artifacts that relate to Clanranald history. 'There are some powers – very strong mystic powers,' he adds, referring to a particular piece of stone that is supposedly invested with the ability to wreak due revenge.

This typical view of the sacred nature of the clan's treasures is even shared by Canon Angus McQueen, who presides over the island's church. 'The Celtic people have always had a great consciousness of the supernatural,' he points out. 'In my early days we believed in ghosts. I still do. We believe in walking past graveyards and saying our prayers when we do it. We believe in the sacred nature of all things that concern the life of the Celtic person.' This sense of religion runs very deep. The Canon adds: 'Even those who perhaps have abandoned God have still got that superstitious side to their natures. This is all very much a part of our make-up. You have to be really born into this feeling of the supernatural governing every moment of your life.'

He points out that much of this reverence is associated with the graveyard, making the grounds of Howmore Chapel, now ruined, all the more signifi-cant. For here lie the remains of many heroes of the Clanranald clan and numerous holy people whose names are known to all the islanders. If anywhere seemed a likely site for a curse, this would be it. Indeed, even the stone columns jut skywards from the derelict building like fingers pointing accusingly at heaven.

Ranald MacDonald is the present and twenty-fourth chieftain of the clan of Clanranald. He is also convinced that the curse is real, although he prefers to call it a 'special protection'. 'The Clanranalds have always been successful up until the end of the clan period in 1746. They were never conquered. Certainly the loyalty of the clan maintained the whole togetherness, and there are many stories about magic-type curses.'

These stories manifest in a dramatic fashion. 'The sad thing is that anybody who tampers with the property of the clan has never really had any advantage and, as often as not, has met with some evilness,' the chieftain explains.

THE STONE OF CLANRANALD

The heart of the Clanranald curse is that any object stolen from their land will find its way back home – after the thief has paid a terrible price for his crime. Typical of the tales that have imbued the curse with an air of

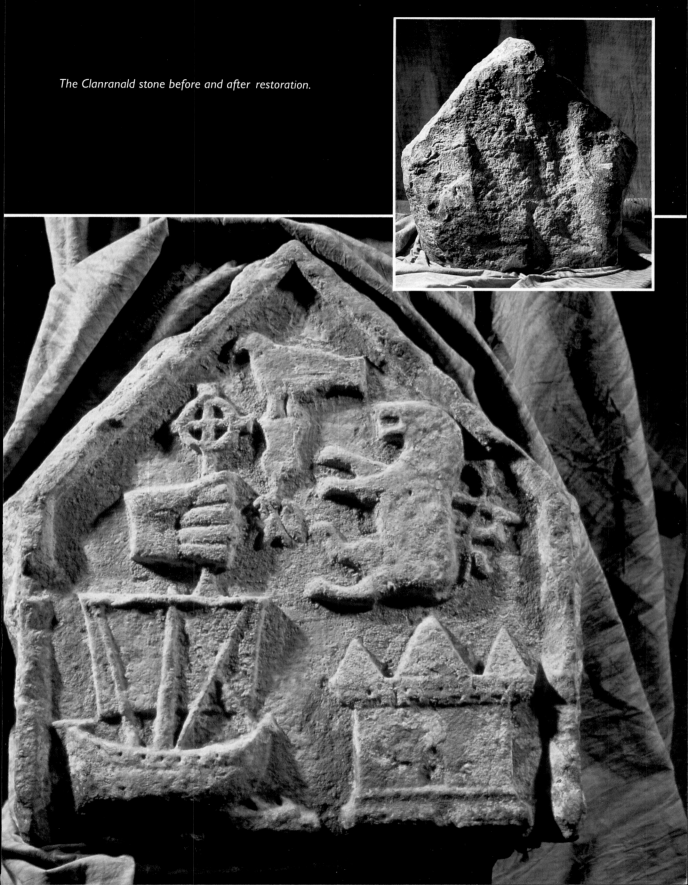

The Clanranald stone before and after restoration.

Bampton in Devon, the scene of a reported timeslip (see Chapter 12). Pictured here during its time as a 'best kept village'.

CURSES OLD AND NEW

It is often mistakenly believed that curses are no more than ancient superstition, but in fact they remain a part of modern life. Visitors to the Isle of Man, another island with strong traditions and a rich Celtic ancestry, still pay homage at 'Fairy Bridge' because they fear that bad luck will strike if they do not do so. In Ireland, belief in the banshee, a wraith-like form whose appearance is always followed by death, remains strong, particularly in rural areas.

The funerary mask of Tutankhamun.

The opening of the tomb of the boy king Tutankhamun in Egypt in 1922 by Howard Carter and the Earl of Caernarvon gave rise to the legend of one of the most famous modern curses. One by one those associated with opening this sacred site died in tragic circumstances. Written on the entrance of the tomb was a warning that such a fate would result if anyone desecrated the tomb. Whilst there are those who argue that there must be a rational explanation – noting that such warnings were often placed on tombs to deter grave robbers in an age when people were more gullible, or even suggesting that some microbe released from the sealed interior may have spread a disease – few would question the power of the curse with anything other than trepidation. Indeed, its power has been said to extend to exhibitions of the artifacts removed from Egypt. In 1979 a planned TV movie about the Earl of Caernarvon's ill-fated expedition was fraught with bad luck and disaster. Star Ian McShane crashed out of the production in an accident on the first day of location shooting.

One view of the power of the curse is that it works by way of belief – almost as if the conviction that the curse is real is enough to make it operate across time. It is well known that in certain tribal cultures people who are 'cursed' by the witchdoctor often die through no apparent physical cause but because they subconsciously appear to submit to the belief in their own doom. Mind – in this case – can be the controlling influence, even deciding between life and death.

conviction is that surrounding the 1745 Jacobite Rebellion, when the British redcoats ended the dominance of the clans.

During this time two soldiers intent on robbery plundered the family graveyard on Loch Shiel and made off with a prize treasure, St Finan's bell. This small bronze bell is believed to be of ancient Celtic date. However, the bell began to ring and nothing the soldiers could do would stop the noise. It alerted the caretaker, who gave chase. The bell, dropped by the fleeing men, was soon returned to its rightful place.

But what happened to the two soldiers? Ranald MacDonald explains: 'St Finan's bell has been taken twice during the last couple of centuries. Both times, I am told, the people who have taken it have met an untimely end.'

However, the most dramatic stories of all seem to support the curse surrounding the Clanranald stone, which sits in the church graveyard, the final resting place of Alan of Moidart, a sixteenth-century chief and clan protector. Nothing symbolizes the clan better than this large, grey, triangular stone. Carved with ancient images that represent the clan, it is the very essence of Clanranald.

In 1708 a copy of the original stone (which was still within the graveyard) was built into the wall of the new Clanranald Castle at Ormacleit, four miles away. Not long afterwards, the castle was burnt to the ground. Yet amidst all the destruction the duplicate Clanranald stone was left undamaged to stand guard over the remains of the clan's heritage.

However, this stone, set unprotected in the grounds of the ruined castle, remains a great temptation to the unwary or foolhardy. As recently as 1990 an attempt was made to challenge the curse and take it away. Very early one morning Ian McCaskill, working at the home farm adjacent to the castle, heard something peculiar. It sounded like a scraping or chipping noise. As Canon McQueen explains: 'He looked towards the castle ruins and there was a man trying to prise out the memorial stone with a hammer and a chisel. Ian just chased him for his life, and that's all we know.'

Good fortune – or perhaps something more sinister – had foiled this latest attempt to steal from the Clanranalds. Once again the family property was safe. As to the consequences for the would-be thief, nobody knows. At any rate, he was never seen again.

An Unpleasant Surprise

In the early winter of 1990, in the wake of the aborted theft of the duplicate stone, a much worse fate was to befall the island. Canon McQueen's niece

THE CURSE OF CORONATION STREET

Another theory about curses links them to mystical sites with powerful earth energies, such as the stone circle sites that dot the Hebrides. Do leys – ancient paths demarking such forces – bond these places together?

In 1983-4 such a ley was thought by some paranormal researchers to pass through a temporary rehearsal studio being used at the Granada television complex in Manchester. It had been built on a site where condemned prisoners were once housed, and some powerful energies were reputedly sensed there. It seems that the unusual energies were felt by the cast of Coronation Street, who were using the rooms at the time. Actress Pat Phoenix, who played Elsie Tanner, said she felt this force in their new accommodation, as did William Roache (Ken Barlow).

One day, as the curse legend took root, I was present with Granada production staff and a psychic in the green room before filming a TV item at the studio. The psychic announced to us all that a death would occur amongst the Coronation Street cast. Not surprisingly we all gave this woman a wide berth, but within days the Street's popular star Peter Dudley, who played Bert Tilsley, did indeed die in unexpected circumstances.

During the time that the Street cast worked in their temporary studio, tragedy struck the show with so much force that speculation about a curse became hard to resist. First, Violet Carson (alias Ena Sharples) and Jack Haworth (Albert Tatlock) both died, although this was not too much of a surprise given their ages. When actress Doris Speed (pub landlady Annie Walker) was forced to leave through ill health, worries mounted. More problems followed as Geoffrey Hughes, who played bin man Eddie Yates, left to take on other roles, as did Pat Phoenix; although her departure was all too short-lived, as she died from a serious illness a couple of years afterwards.

By the time Barbara Knox (newsagent Rita Fairclough) became very ill with a serious virus, there was open talk in the paranormal community that maybe the energy being sensed at this site had consolidated itself into a curse. More gloom followed with the death of Bernard Youens (Stan Ogden).

I have no way of knowing if this curse was more than just a freak combination of tragedies. But I can personally attest to the strangeness of the site. Coronation Street has gone from strength to strength since leaving its temporary home. If there ever was a curse of Coronation Street, it has thankfully now disappeared.

Cathy Haith of the British Museum with the Clanranald stone.

was visiting South Uist and asked her uncle to show her the famous Moidart memorial stone. However, when they arrived, something was amiss. 'She said, "It's not here,"' the Canon recalls. 'I said, "Of course it's there. Just move along around the corner." But it wasn't there.' The greatest treasure of the Clanranald clan had indeed disappeared.

Canon McQueen goes on: 'When the locals heard the stone had gone they were upset, because they hate our graveyards to be desecrated in any way. There was a mild sense of shock.'

Ranald MacDonald also describes the aftermath, 'When I first heard the stone had gone missing I felt very sorry – both for myself and my family. I offered a reward of £500 in the hope that it might stimulate something.'

The whole island was abuzz with talk, but despite the generous reward, nobody could discover what had happened. The Canon adds: 'We alerted all the neighbouring crofters and none of them had heard or seen anything. Yet a couple of days later one of the crofters showed me a mark where the stone had obviously been dragged from the graveyard all the way to the parking place outside the church.'

Somehow this heavy stone, three feet high and weighing over a third of a ton had been tugged from the earth, dragged bodily across the graveyard and presumably hoisted into the back of a vehicle. Ranald MacDonald notes: 'They must have used a small crowbar or something. I mean, it is within the wit of man, but it would have been quite a difficult, determined journey.'

Did an ancient curse claim this man's life?

By Deborah Sherwood and Julian Newman

FOR generations, the Hebridean islanders of South Uist feared the legendary curse of the Lords and Kings of Clanranald.

Ancient folklore, widely accepted to this day by the people of the tiny island, has it that anyone who desecrated the clan's ancient gravestone would be doomed to an early death.

Today many of South Uist's 1,800 population believe the curse has struck.

They say it is responsible for the death of Lawren Maben, a young Canadian who defied the legend and made off with the Clanranald stone, carrying it to his home in London as a bizarre souvenir.

An extract from Sunday Express, *dated 9 April 1995, picturing Lawren Maben.*

Yet still the questions nagged. Who had stolen this priceless artifact? What did they want with it? And why had the curse failed to stop them?

A MISADVENTURE

At the end of February 1995 Cathy Haith was working at her office in the British Museum in London, when a most unusual request came from the information desk. Cathy, who works at the museum as a curator, describes what happened: 'They told me there was a gentleman there who urgently wanted to see someone. They said he was a little upset. So I spoke to him over the phone and he came down to the department and showed me a photo of a carved stone which he said was in a nearby flat in Euston.'

Cathy was not an expert in this type of medieval stonework, but immediately recognized the importance of the find. The man indicated that its origin was Scotland, so she sent the photograph and some sketches to Historic Scotland and the National Museum of Antiquities. Very rapidly the news came back that this object had been missing for five years almost to the day. It was the stolen Clanranald stone.

The man who had come to the museum was called David Maben, and he explained to Cathy what he knew about the find. 'He said that his son had been on holiday some years previously in South Uist and had found it in a field and then brought it back to London,' Cathy says. 'It had remained in his flat ever since.' Whether he had deliberately set out to steal the stone will never be known.

The reason why David Maben was in London at that time was that he had come for his son's funeral. Thirty-three-year-old Lawren Maben had been found dead in his tiny bedsit. The circumstances were unclear and could only be described by the coroner as 'misadventure'. Just a few feet from his body stood the Clanranald stone, propped up against the window.

HOME AT LAST

On 10 June 1995 the ferry from Oban sailed into harbour on South Uist. The whole island was waiting for its cargo. A piper played a sad lament as the Clanranald stone returned home at last. Ranald MacDonald was delighted when he first heard the news about the discovery of the stone, but his excitement was soon tempered. 'I was a little concerned and saddened,' he said. 'I was also slightly spooked by the fact of the boy's death. It rather brought reminiscences of various things I have heard and the mystery of the clan.' Canon McQueen was less surprised. 'We all expected something like this,' he adds. 'But when the stone was found in these circumstances, I said that is the sort of thing that might have happened in the Celtic world, but not in the heart of London.'

12

A SLIP IN TIME

O ne of the most exciting themes in science fiction is the idea that one day we may travel through time. All the great pioneer writers in this field, from Mark Twain to H G Wells, adopted the idea and hundreds of movies about it have been made.

But is time travel just a romantic notion unsupported by any real evidence? There are those who would say otherwise, based on their first-hand experiences. These are people who have undergone what paranormal researchers call a 'timeslip' and believe that they have literally travelled through time.

Timeslips most often take the witness back into the past; although a small number of voyages into the future have also been recorded. Unsuspecting victims enter a scene that once really did take place – but, unlike those who may see a ghost in a haunted room, they find themselves not only watching but actually taking part in the activity that surrounds them. They are not mere observers of another time – they have travelled there, as surely as if snatched out of today's reality and relocated in another age.

These are amongst the rarest forms of supernatural experience, with no more than one or two cases a year being recorded. They are also inherently fantastic and difficult for many sceptics to accept. However, to those who go through the shift in time frame they generally represent one of the most amazing experiences that they will ever have. For if you find yourself visiting another age, it can be both real and terrifying.

VILLAGE GREENERY

One summer evening in 1993, Alf and Eileen Roberts were returning from a holiday trip. They were driving through the leafy lanes of mid Devon,

BAMPTON — DEVON

A postcard showing Bampton as it was in the late '70s.

heading for a hotel in Dunster, Somerset, where they were staying. Gradually they realized that they were not exactly certain where they were and were in danger of running late. 'We found ourselves lost and stopped by the green at the top of this village to decide which way to go,' Alf Roberts explains.

As they consulted the map and tried to agree upon the right direction, they noticed the unusual prettiness of their surroundings. 'On the green in the middle of a flower bed was this huge wooden sign,' he adds. 'It was varnished, highly polished and said something like "Award for the best kept village, Bampton, 1976."'

Eileen agrees. 'I couldn't believe my eyes. It was so brilliant and the tubs of flowers and window boxes – everything – was just one mass of colour. It was really lovely.'

After debating what to do next, they drove on through the village, noting the unusual pinkish orange paintwork of the stone houses. Reaching the far end of Bampton they turned around to head back and stopped when they met an old man walking up the hill. He directed them out of the village, and they remember leaving through an avenue of trees whose branches had grown towards one another from either side of the road to create a tunnel. Underneath, it was so dark that Alf had to switch on his headlight beams, even though it was not yet dusk.

So impressed were they by this award-winning village that they decided to revisit the next day and take some photographs. But it was not to be so simple as that. Alf recalls: 'We stopped by the green where we had stopped the night before and the sign had gone. The flower bed had gone. It was just grass.' Puzzled, they drove on, but the entire village had altered in a fundamental way that was difficult to imagine.

Eileen describes the situation: 'All the tubs and the flower pots and the hanging baskets – everything – had gone.' She added: 'We couldn't believe it

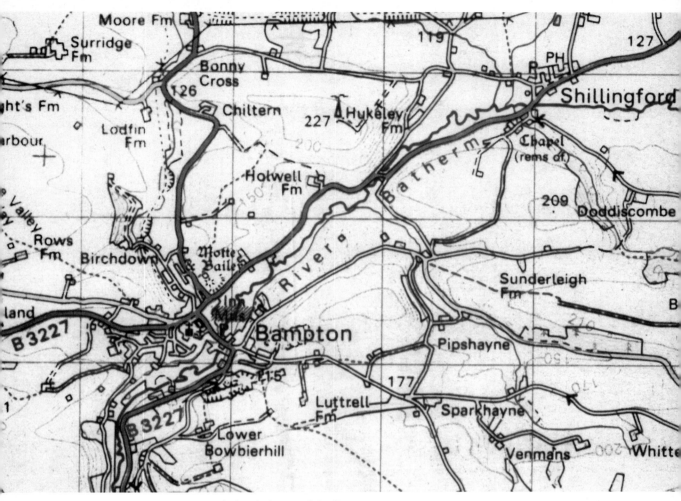

A detailed map of the Bampton area.

was the same village, but we knew it was. Even the house walls were now a dull slate grey. All the colour had vanished overnight.'

These were not the only mysteries. Both Alf and Eileen remember that when they stopped to read the map the night before, they had accidentally set fire to it with a dropped cigarette. The smoke had filled the car. Yet when they looked at the map again, they saw it was not even singed.

Then there was the problem with time itself. 'When we first arrived in the village we checked the time,' Alf says. 'It was half past seven. When we eventually turned round and went out of the village it was still half past seven by my watch and the clock on the car dashboard. We backtracked and did the same thing the next day. It took us thirteen minutes.'

So why did time appear to stand still when they visited Bampton on that first night? It was as if they had never been there at all – at least, in our reality – but had instead passed into some sort of time warp, viewing the village as it once must have been.

Had they seen the Bampton of seventeen years earlier when it was in a state of full bloom and it had won its best-kept village award?

NO ROOM AT THE INN

Len and Cynthia Gisby and Geoff and Pauline Simpson were firm friends. It was no surprise when in 1979 they all decided to take a late summer holiday together. The plan was to take the ferry from near their homes in Dover, Kent, and travel through France, sharing the driving and travelling overnight to reach their Spanish holiday destination the next day. Then, after two weeks of early autumn sunshine, they would set off back for England by the same route.

Everything went well until the end of that first long and hot day in France. Len wanted to continue and take advantage of the clear road, but Cynthia and Pauline were growing very weary. Apart from brief stops they had been car-bound for twelve hours and so, somewhere near Montelimar, it was agreed that they should try and find a place that offered a bed for the night, an evening meal and breakfast.

They came off the *autoroute* at Montelimar North, where a sign indicated there was a motel. Len got out and went to investigate. The receptionist said that unfortunately there was only one room left, but suggested that the visitors try the little back road towards Avignon. There they should come upon a smaller hotel that might have vacancies.

AN OLD-FASHIONED PLACE

Cynthia remembers what this little side road was like. 'It became very quiet. There was fencing along the road. Pauline and I laughed at the old photographs and posters that were stuck on the wall – one advertising a circus.'

As the road became just a narrow, cobbled track, they began to worry that they were not going to find the hotel. Then a long building, like a barn with an extra storey on top, loomed ahead. Len stopped and went to the door.

He remembers what he found inside: 'It was actually a restaurant, and so I

Holiday snapshots taken in Spain –
the photograph on the right shows
Len and Cynthia Gisby on the left and
Pauline and Geoff Simpson on the right.

went in and asked the chap behind the counter – a wooden counter – if he
had accommodation.' It took a while to get him to understand, but eventually, despite his limited French, Len discovered that they did have two rooms.
Everyone in the car was relieved.

Pauline Simpson took her overnight bag from the car up to the bedroom.
'The room was weird,' she says. 'The sheets were bleached white. They were
very thick and large and we didn't have pillows – just a round bolster that
went right across the top of the bed.' There was only a dim light in the room
– no electrical switches. Later, to climb the stairs, they were even given
candles! The bathroom was even odder – at the end of a long corridor and
huge. But the antique bath was sunk into the floor and the soap was stuck
into a metal spike on the wall. The windows to the rooms were just as unusual
as everything else in this building, with slatted shutters but no glass.

Downstairs in the dining room Len and Cynthia Gisby were feeling equally
bemused. A woman in an old-fashioned dress and a fringed cap asked them
what they all wanted. They recognized the word *oeuf*, meaning egg, and
Cynthia ordered that. The women ended up with egg and sautéed potatoes
and the men had steak for their meal. Even the cutlery was strangely heavy

and basic-looking. Len was particularly impressed by the beer – in quaint old jars with stoppers, and like nothing they had tasted before. Everyone enjoyed their meal.

In the next room some rustic-looking Frenchmen were sitting around a large wooden table and, as Cynthia comments: 'We just thought it was old rural France and had a laugh. We thought it was part and parcel of the holiday.'

They did not stay long in the restaurant as they were all desperately tired. None of them remembers dreaming and they all fell quickly asleep. The road outside was completely devoid of passing traffic, but Len recalled a whistling or hooting that may have come from a nearby railway line.

BREAKFAST WITH TRIMMINGS

The next morning they all awoke early as there was another long day driving ahead. It looked like being a scorcher again. They were simply delighted with this 'theme hotel', as they saw it, and wondered why the tourist brochures had not discovered its charms.

There was a delay before they could go down for breakfast, as the hotel manager – wearing a thick white shirt with a very old-style collar – was mopping the floor. So the men seized the opportunity to take some pictures. 'Stay there,' Len told the women, as they were framed in a window opening. Then both he and Geoff took photographs with their respective cameras.

After loading the car Len and Geoff joined their wives, who had now managed to get into the dining room for breakfast. This was to turn into a spectacle. 'The bread was very heavy and coarse,' Cynthia remembers. 'It was sort of brown like in wartime and very sweet.' The coffee was black and sludge-like too, Geoff recalls.

Then in marched two policemen. Len recollects: 'While we were at breakfast these two *gendarmes* came in. I had never seen anything like the uniforms before. They were very dark, and they had gaiters up to their knees. One had a very tall pillar-box hat on.' Geoff basically agreed, adding that he thought the uniforms were dark blue. They had seen *gendarmes* on their route south and none had worn clothing like this. Again the four holidaymakers assumed that it was a custom peculiar to this rural part of France.

Then a young woman came into the hotel, dressed in mauve, who looked even stranger. Pauline says: 'She had a skirt that came right down to her ankles. The bottom of the skirt was uneven. She had weird shoe things on that had buttons all up the side. It was as though she had been to a fancy dress party.' But at 7 a.m. in the middle of nowhere that seemed unlikely! The woman and the *gendarmes* engaged in lively chat as the visitors looked on in mild amusement.

THE ROAD TO AVIGNON

Len reckoned that they had driven about two miles off the motorway near Montelimar, and he wondered if there was an easier way to continue towards Avignon. He decided to ask one of the policemen. 'I said "*autoroute*?" Then I said "Avignon?"' The *gendarme* looked back at the Englishman completely baffled, as if he had never heard the word *autoroute* before. He did describe a way to reach Avignon but when the two couples consulted their map later in the car it seemed to be a very long way round. So they decided to retrace their steps of the previous night.

Before leaving, Len went to settle the bill with the *patron*. 'I asked him how much it was and he got a piece of paper and wrote on it "19". And I said, "19 francs?" He nodded. I said, "No, it's more than that." So the policeman joined in and he said, "Non, finis, 19 francs."'

Len told the others, who were standing nearby, what had happened. Pauline remembers: 'He said it was about £2.50 for all four of us, which was ridiculous. Cynthia stood there and I laughed at her actions as she mimed that we had dinner last night and slept upstairs. She looked so funny trying to make them see that we should be paying more.'

Nothing would get through to the *patron*. The incredibly low bill stood – even though it worked out at about 60 pence per person for bed, breakfast and evening meal. As Len says: 'So I gave him a twenty-franc note in modern currency and said, "Let's get away quick."'

The delighted guests hurried out to their car and drove away.

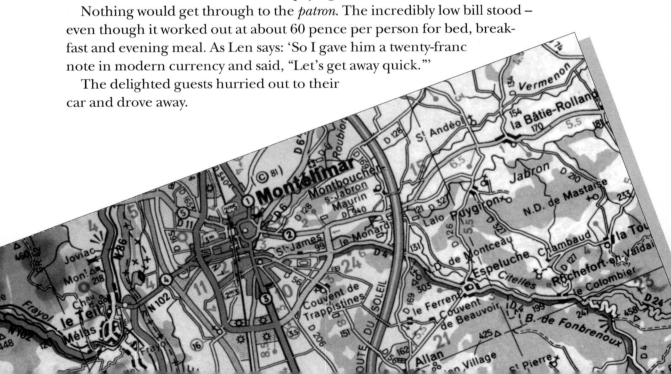

TIMESLIPS: THE FRENCH CONNECTION

The records of paranormal research contain several dozen cases where people appear to have travelled back in time, although none is as extraordinary as the experience of the Gisbys and Simpsons, and none involves so many witnesses. Neither has an overnight stay in another dimension been recorded before. However, intriguingly, France features quite often in these peculiar accounts.

The earliest-known timeslip involved two English gentlewomen schoolteachers who visited the Palace of Versailles near Paris in 1901 and stumbled upon what they took to be a costume party. They wandered around the gardens and met people in old-fashioned clothes, including a woman painting at an easel. It was only afterwards that they began to suspect that something very strange was going on.

It transpired that there had been no party that day. Furthermore, when the women left the garden things seemed to return to normal. Investigations which they carried out for their book, entitled *An Adventure*, suggested that they had slipped back in time over a hundred years and that the woman by the easel might even have been Marie Antoinette.

Two more English women tourists were in France in August 1951 when another timeslip occurred. They were staying at the Channel port of Dieppe when they heard a series of explosions, gunfire and overhead aircraft. So persistent and perplexing was it that they kept a detailed log of these unseen events, which proved useful when the Society for Psychical Research later checked out their case.

There had been an Allied raid on Dieppe nine years before this mysterious occurrence – but nobody else in the town seems to have heard the phenomena that these women experienced in 1951. The only logical explanation seems to be that they somehow had an auditory replay of those traumatic events which had been transposed through nearly a decade of time.

THE JOURNEY HOME

That night in such a wonderful hotel had got their holiday off to a terrific start. After the sun and relaxation of Spain there was never any doubt where they were going to stay to break their long journey home, particularly when the weather deteriorated. So two weeks later, they came off the *autoroute* and found the big motel at Montelimar. Moments later they were on the back road seeking the marvellous theme hotel again.

'We couldn't find the place,' Geoff explains. 'We turned around, went back to the motel car park, went down the little road again – we must have done this three or four times. By now we were getting rather cross with one another and the hotel definitely wasn't there.'

He accused Len of putting them on to the wrong road. Len disputed this – but could they have taken a wrong turning? Geoff is adamant, in retrospect, that this was not possible. 'I was on the right road. There was only one road out of there – it had to be the right road.' Pauline had been unwell that day and they were desperate to find the hotel. The red wall with its old posters was on this road – so they knew this was the same route they had followed two weeks earlier. They even found the lay-by where they had pulled off the road.

'But there was nothing opposite it,' Pauline insists. The hotel which had been in this precise spot only days before had now simply vanished. As Cynthia added: 'What struck us was that the trees down this road had been small the time before. Now they were great big trees.'

What on earth was going on? They speculated about the hotel going out of business because of the absurdly low prices, but knew that all trace of it could not be obliterated so quickly.

They were forced to drive into Lyon to stay the night. Here they ate only a sandwich and the bill came to 247 francs – thirteen times what they had paid at the disappearing hotel.

Some years later they drove back through France to try to find their dream hotel again. They easily located the lay-by, but even with the help of the local tourist board they failed to find the extraordinarily cheap residence in which they had stayed. It was as if they had spent the night in a phantom hotel – one that existed only in the past.

IN THE PICTURE

Even after arriving home in Kent the Gisbys and the Simpsons were not convinced that anything supernatural had occurred in France. They were puzzled as to why they could not find the hotel, but they all knew that they had stayed in it. So there had to be some explanation. Besides which, both couples had taken photographs that would prove this point.

Geoff's camera was a very basic model. It took twelve exposures and was of the point-and-shoot variety. Twelve prints and negatives were returned by the processors – but none showed the hotel. Geoff says: 'I knew I had taken a photograph and I had seen Len take some. I knew I should have had the hotel on the roll of film that was developed. It wasn't there. I was really surprised – and shocked.'

When Len's film was processed, his photographs had not come out either. He says: 'I changed the film at the Spanish border. There should have been three pictures of the hotel but they were not there. I got all the numbered prints and negatives. There were no blanks.'

'It's unreal,' was all his wife could think of adding. According to the sequence of numbers printed on the negative strip, the images of the hotel were never registered, although some scratch marks on the film suggested that his camera might have tried to wind on.

Not surprisingly, as Cynthia says, 'We never discussed it after that. We kept quiet about it.'

Geoff remarked: 'There was something wrong, but I did not know what it was. It was totally new to me.' He added that it frightened his wife, and so they decided to remain silent.

THE PHANTOM HOTEL

The story came out by accident about four years later, when a friend shared the tale with a local newspaper journalist. Not long afterwards, in July 1985, I met Geoff and Pauline Simpson when they briefly returned north to Geoff's childhood home in Rochdale.

I discussed their case at some length. Indeed, Geoff was even hypnotically regressed by a Manchester psychiatrist in order to relive the timeslip – a unique experiment that was set up by researcher Harry Harris. But although Geoff recalled the experience with emotion and in considerable detail, little new detail was added. Pauline still seemed too concerned by her experience to respond to hypnosis.

At this time Geoff was a railway worker and Pauline a cleaner at a local social club. Both were in their mid-forties. They were very down to earth about it. Geoff told me: 'If anyone else had told us this story we would have laughed. We still chuckled about it ourselves, but we knew it had to be true.'

One thing I discovered was that the weather on the night of this remarkable story was very hot and sticky, with a great deal of electricity crackling in the atmosphere. This has been reported before in connection with timeslip cases and may suggest that there is some sort of natural force field that occurs from time to time in certain places and can cause breaches in space and time. In addition, the area where these events occurred is notorious in France for paranormal activity. In the Vaucluse and Provence regions to the south and east of Montelimar and Avignon there have been countless reports of time anomalies, strange lights in the sky, apparitional figures and electrical effects on car engines and headlights.

Of course, I also asked Geoff and Pauline about my more cautionary concerns, such as how the hotel owner could accept 1979 currency if – as was being speculated – he really existed in the distant past? Indeed, how come nobody at the hotel was astonished by the modern car parked outside? It would presumably look like something out of science fiction to a person from an earlier age. Nor had it escaped my attention that the town of Avignon was wonderfully poetic – given that this is phonetically pronounced in a similar way to 'having you on' !

To be fair to the Simpsons, they answered me very simply and with apparent honesty and did not try to come up with explanations. 'You tell us what the answer is. We only know what happened,' Geoff pointed out in reply.

Len says that the problem with the currency is something he has thought about many times since 1979. Of the hotel keeper's decision to take the money without evident concern, he can only say: 'He accepted it and that was it.' Of course, they did leave quite rapidly afterwards, giving the hotelier little chance to question the modern twenty-franc note, but Len fully realizes the dilemma that this poses.

FINDING THE RIGHT TIME

In 1995 Pauline adds that she is still perturbed by what happened that night. 'I know I was there – I lived it. But I don't want to remember. I try to block it out.' Generally the Simpsons have been more reluctant to recall their experience than their friends; although, like the Gisbys, they stressed that they did not make up this story and have purposely made no money out of it as they could so easily have done. Len and Cynthia, on the other hand, seem more willing to speculate about a paranormal explanation. In fact they have done some detective work of their own.

Len happened to know a French dressmaker who lived nearby, and he and

And the pictures were blank

GRAHAM SMITH reports on an amazing story of a trip to a French hotel.

Len and Cynthia later described what had happened to a French friend of theirs, a dressmaker, who told them something that unnerved them. She said the clothing worn by the woman who came into the hotel that morning was of the early 1900s style, and that the uniforms worn by the two gendarmes have not been worn by gendarmes since 1905. Len and Cynthia

from t. the ho
But Pauline and C find o pened ago.
" What weird, not kr it.
Th

An extract from the Dover Express, dated 11 February 1983.

his wife have taken the opportunity to discuss the case with her. Cynthia described the woman's mauve dress which they saw at breakfast time, and Len added details about the *gendarmes'* uniforms. After looking at pictures in old books which this woman possessed, Len says: 'We found that these uniforms were used, but not after 1905.' This fitted in very well with the style of the woman's clothing, which also appeared to date from that same era.

Another discovery added to this evidence. Len points out, after consulting various old records: 'The price we paid for accommodation was in the middle of the range given by the Thomas Cook travel agency, and corresponds for around that time of 1905.' In other words, all of these indications suggest that the hotel they visited was set in a time just after the turn of the century.

It does seem difficult to conceive of any other explanation for what the Simpsons and the Gisbys say took place. If they are telling the truth – as we have no reason to disbelieve – then it would seem likely that in some incredible way they were able to spend a night living in the past. Of course, this poses huge problems. What if someone in 1905 had seen their car and used it to invent a modern horseless carriage? Would history have been changed? More dramatically, and according to an old adage used by physicists to 'prove' that time travel is impossible, what if the mother of one of these four people had been staying in France in 1905 whilst still a child herself? What if an action that the time travellers accidentally performed brought about that woman's death? If they had killed one of their own parents, then the unfortunate (and still unconceived) time traveller could never have been born, of course, and so would not have existed to go back from 1979 to 1905 and thus kill their mother – the event which created this paradox!

The logic of this hypothetical dilemma goes round in circles and is mind-numbing. It is not difficult to see why science finds it difficult to concede the possibility of time travelling. Indeed, the consequences of someone being able to live in the past – even for just one night – are so awesome that they shake the very basis of time, space, cause and effect, and probably demolish modern physics. No wonder sceptics find timeslips so uncomfortable.

On the other hand, if just one case is ever provable, then it represents one of the most important phenomena in the paranormal universe. A timeslip may, quite literally, change the world.

PART SIX

UFOs

It has been called the greatest mystery of the space age and remains one of the most talked about phenomena on earth.

Whether you believe that UFOs are alien visitors, some sort of illusion or advanced military projects, the evidence depends crucially on eyewitness testimony. Someone says that they have seen a strange light. Should you believe them? Are they reliable? Could they be mistaken - was it just a weather balloon?

Sadly, there is often no hard evidence to back these stories up. The world remains unconvinced.

But there is a secret history to the UFO mystery. One that involves extremely credible witnesses, trained to observe things in the sky. It has a catalogue of amazing encounters, many of which have powerful support – evidence in the form of radar, movie film and scientific investigation.

13

EYES ON THE SKIES

There have probably always been unidentified flying objects. When ancient man first gazed at the heavens and observed countless millions of twinkling stars he could have had no idea what they were. So he invented a mythology to surround them. This was the human race's first attempt at turning the unknown into less of a problem – first by giving it awe-inspiring names and then by striving to understand it.

There were other wonders to be faced. The rainbow, for example, was a puzzling spectre that appeared from time to time in the daylight sky. At first this, too, was deified to make it palatable. Our ancestors gave it god-like attributes and spectacular names. Then, as the ancient civilizations developed basic science, observation took over. It was realized that rainbows formed when rain and sunlight were present. It took thousands of years before the physics of the rainbow could be deciphered, but eventually one more UFO succumbed to the march of science.

You may think such analogies trite: they do not represent the true complexity of the UFO mystery, with its baffling alien objects zipping across the skies and seen by credible observers. But, in fact, all UFOs are just unidentified phenomena in the skies. They are mysteries waiting to be solved when we reach the point in human progress that allows such a solution to be found.

Things that once were UFOs but are now IFOs (that is, identified flying objects) point the way that many of today's mysteries will eventually go. For although we may think we know everything about the universe we live in we are really still in kindergarten. Each year we discover answers to questions that last year we did not even think to ask.

Some of the phenomena which the ancient Romans and Greeks saw and considered to be UFOs are fully explained by modern science. The dazzling lights which they named as burning shields or golden lances – using words familiar to their society – were just meteors, comets or ball lightning.

Today, in the space age, we too use words to camouflage our own lack of understanding. We call our UFOs flying saucers, giant cigars, even alien spacecraft to side-step the fact that we don't know what they are. Our mistake is to delude ourselves that using glamorous phrases can explain what UFOs are. All they can ever do is mask our uncertainty.

LYING SAUCERS

It is impossible to say when UFOs were first reported, but we can develop a working picture through the many sightings made by pilots. Pilots are trained observers who know how to identify what is in the sky and to chart their way through problems. Moreover, since they spend a great deal of their working lives above cloud level, often at night, they are in the optimum position to see UFOs. If there are things out there which are puzzling in origin, then the one group of people expected to see them would be pilots.

American Kenneth Arnold was flying his private aircraft over the Cascade Mountains of Washington State on 24 June 1947 when he spotted a series of objects moving between two peaks. He carefully measured their motion and speed and assumed they were military jets of some unfamiliar type. But he was baffled by their aerodynamic capabilities and remarkable shape – something like a crescent with a bite cut out.

Arnold reported the sighting over the radio, and on reaching his destination was greeted by a swarm of journalists. He explained that the objects had moved 'like a saucer skipping across water' – a curious phrase, meant to liken their motion to a flat stone that a child might bounce across the surface of a pond. He certainly never intended it to describe a saucer-like shape.

What Arnold really saw will forever be debated. Some tried to establish that it was a mirage of the mountain peaks; others that they were military planes and he mistook their speed and distance. As a sighting it was neither especially spectacular nor did it offer any proof. But it did change the world. An enterprising reporter, slightly misinterpreting Arnold's words, invented the phrase 'flying saucer'. Everyone started to look for them, and many saw them. Science fiction movies depicted how alien invaders would arrive in saucer-shaped crafts. A new craze was born – all based upon a simple mistake.

PROJECT SAUCER

By the autumn of 1947 the US government had little choice but to launch a military-style investigation – in secret, of course, as this was the beginning of the cold war and at first there were genuine fears that the UFOs might be Soviet secret weapons. The investigation was nicknamed 'Project Saucer'. But as soon as it was launched it faced a huge crisis, when the UFOs claimed their first victim.

Pilot Kenneth Arnold, who reported seeing unidentified flying objects over the Cascade Mountains of Washington State on 24 June 1947.

There had been sightings of a light in the sky over Kentucky from about 1.15 p.m. on 7 January 1948. The control tower at Godman Field USAF airbase was contacted by the police, who were receiving reports from people across a 200-mile radius. Staff at the base scoured the heavens with binoculars, looking for the UFO.

At the same time Captain Thomas Mantell, leader of a four-plane team on a routine ferrying mission, flew over the field in his F-51 aircraft. Although Mantell and the other pilots had just passed through the area of sky where the UFO was situated, none of them had seen anything. However, Godman asked them to turn around and investigate. This they did, minus one aircraft which was low on fuel and so went on to its destination.

By around 2.45 p.m. Mantell and his two wingmen had climbed to 20,000 feet in the search for the UFO. As their aircraft were not fitted with oxygen masks it was dangerous to climb any higher. The other pilots tried to warn their leader to break off, but he was last seen at 22,500 feet – still climbing.

DEATH IN THE AFTERNOON

The air-to-ground communications between Mantell and Godman Field were not recorded, but from later reconstruction it is known that he described seeing a light and said he would level off at 25,000 feet. He then reported an object 'above and ahead of me' and stated at about 3.15 p.m. that it was 'metallic and tremendous in size'. He claimed he was still trying to close in but was not getting any nearer.

One of the wingmen made brief visual contact with the object before breaking off the chase. He said it was still way above them, shaped like a 'teardrop' and it 'seemed fluid'. Within minutes of landing to refuel at Godman he was up in the air once more in pursuit of Captain Mantell, with whom all contact had now been lost. The UFO finally disappeared from the sight of ground observers at Godman at 3.45 p.m. It was drifting slowly westwards and had been in view for over two hours.

The wreck of Thomas Mantell's F-51 was found about an hour later. An eye witness had seen it plunge vertically from the sky and break up as a result of the aerodynamic forces. Mantell died instantly – his watch stopping at 3.18 p.m. The ground witness did not see any UFO. There was never any doubt what killed the pilot: he had lost consciousness, presumably due to lack of oxygen at such a great height; his plane, out of control, went into a steep dive and his fate was sealed.

The real problem facing Project Sign, as it was officially named, was that its directors did not have a clue as to the origin of this UFO. Yet they were under orders from the Pentagon not to cause panic by implying that Mantell had tangled with an alien spaceship. Fortunately, they had just appointed a young astronomer from Ohio, Dr J. Allen Hynek, as adviser to the project. He showed that the planet Venus was in more or less the same position in the sky as the dim light seen from Godman tower. It was difficult to view this planet in daylight, but if you were scouring the sky with binoculars looking for a UFO you might just pick it up. So the UFO was Venus – or, at least, that was the explanation issued to the public.

CONSPIRACY OF SILENCE

The way in which this highly dubious solution was foisted on to the public provoked suspicions about a government plot to hide the truth. In the Mantell case the cover-up was not to hide the fact that the pilot had died at the hands of an alien spacecraft. It was to obscure the fact that the US Air Force was completely bemused by what had taken place.

In fact, the truth about Mantell's death was suspected in 1948 by the USAF investigators but could not be proven by them – through no fault of their own. They had sensibly speculated that the UFO was a high-altitude balloon, but could not find one that should have been in the area.

To anyone familiar with UFOs the balloon solution to this case is obvious. Clearly, the object was at a great height because of the wide spread of witnesses on the ground, and the very slow drifting motion (in line with the wind direction at that altitude) is also characteristic. The phrases used to describe the object have all been used many times by witnesses who have seen a high-flying balloon. It does indeed resemble a large, silvery metallic teardrop or ice cream cone-shaped mass.

Sadly, it took many years for this truth to emerge. The UFO was indeed a balloon, part of the US Navy's Skyhook project initiated by the US Navy. This was top secret in 1948 and the staff at Godman were unaware of the test flights. Had they known of them, they could probably have saved Mantell's life.

It was as recently as 1993 that UFOlogist Barry Greenwood, using declassified material, was able to establish with reasonable certainty the launching-point and flight path of the balloon that traversed Kentucky on 7 January 1948. It had innocently created one of the greatest legends in UFO history.

HOISTING THE MAINBRACE

During the late 1940s and early 1950s there were further encounters between UFOs and aircraft above the USA. Whilst there were sightings elsewhere, most other countries regarded it as an American craziness. However, that attitude changed in a few short weeks during the summer of 1952.

Initially it was a wave of sightings in Washington DC that provoked attention. Civil and military pilots observed the lights. Radar stations at both a USAF base and Washington's main airport tracked them. Project Blue Book, as the US government's UFO investigation had now been named, was sent into a tailspin.

In Britain, Prime Minister Winston Churchill was sufficiently impressed by the intelligence reports to send a memo on 28 July to Lord Cherwell, Secretary of State for Air, requesting full details of what was going on. He was told that most UFOs were cases of mistaken identity and there was nothing to worry about regarding the rest. This line came direct from the US study. But between 19 and 21 September that year UFOs made their presence felt locally.

The scene was Operation Mainbrace, a combined services NATO exercise based on eastern England. At 10.53 on the first morning an RAF Meteor jet was pursued by a UFO over Dishforth in Yorkshire. It was also seen by observers on the ground, and changed direction with rapid movements. On the 20th, a US aircraft carrier in the North Sea was buzzed by UFOs. Finally, the next day, six RAF jets closed in on a silvery UFO and watched it streak away from them at an incredible speed.

OFFICIALLY A SECRET

Ralph Noyes, who ran the relevant department at the Ministry of Defence for several years from 1969, reports how at the time of these early 1950s events he was on the staff of Air Chief Marshal Cochran and sat in on Cabinet-level discussions. There was great concern about what was happening.

On 13 January 1953 the British government issued a signal coded FC/S.45485. This has never been made public, but, from references in later memos that were released, it seems to have been aimed at preventing RAF pilots talking about their UFO sightings. A memo dated 16 December that year states: 'It is essential that the information should be examined at the Air Ministry and that its release should be controlled officially.' Pilots were also ordered 'not to communicate to anyone other than official persons any

172

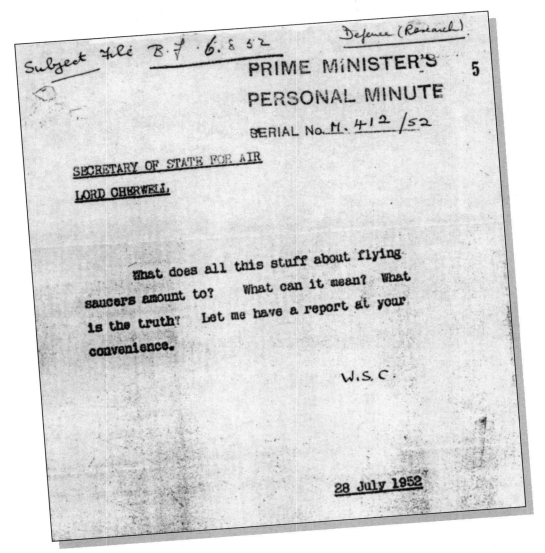

Subject File B.7.6.8 52

Defence (Research)

PRIME MINISTER'S PERSONAL MINUTE

5

SERIAL No. M. 412/52

SECRETARY OF STATE FOR AIR

LORD CHERWELL

What does all this stuff about flying saucers amount to? What can it mean? What is the truth? Let me have a report at your convenience.

W.S.C.

28 July 1952

Winston Churchill's memo to the Secretary of State for Air, Lord Cherwell.

information about phenomena they have observed'. Just how many encounters occurred over in Britain is therefore difficult to estimate. However, retired fliers have talked about their experiences often decades later and official documents normally cease to be kept secret after thirty years.

Ralph Noyes tells us that when he took on his top Ministry job he was shown gun-camera film captured by RAF jets during such chases in the 1950s. This included a pursuit over East Anglia in August 1956 when a UFO was seen from the ground, from the air and on ground and airborne radar! None of this has ever been released even though, Noyes says, it only showed fuzzy lights ahead of the plane. However, the existence of this film certainly confirms that the RAF encountered baffling objects during this period.

THE GOOSE BAY AFFAIR

Military pilots were not the only ones to encounter UFOs during the 1950s. One of the most remarkable cases involved BOAC, then Britain's premier international airline. The Stratocruiser Sierra Charlie set off from New York at 9.03 GMT on 29 June 1954, bound for London. Its captain was James Howard, first officer Lee Boyd, navigator H McDonnell and stewardess Daphne O'Reilley. They were all to take part in one of the most dramatic aerial encounters to date. It happened just after midnight GMT on 30 June at 19,000 feet, when the plane was crossing Canada and heading for Goose Bay, Labrador, where they would make a brief refuelling stop.

Captain James Howard in 1954.

Captain Howard first saw the object 'moving off our port beam at a lower altitude at a distance of maybe five miles'. It was a large dark cigar shape, and six small black ovals seemed to mill about it like animals feeding off their mother. One by one the crew were called to watch the phenomenon, which moved up slowly through thin cloud towards them. When tracked down and interviewed for the first time a quarter of a century later by UFOlogist Barry King, navigator McDonnell reported how the crew swopped stories in an attempt to find a viable explanation. Nobody came up with one.

The idea that the UFO was a shadow from their own fuselage was contemplated but the angle of flight seemed to rule this out, even though the sun was setting at the time. Captain Howard suggested that the object appeared to change shape and was rather amorphous. McDonnell wondered if the changing angles of the sun's rays might have created this illusion.

After watching the UFO for about fifteen minutes Lee Boyd called Goose Bay, on Captain Howard's instructions, and the airbase sent up an interceptor, codenamed Pinto One. But the Canadian Air Force F-94 never saw the UFO. Before the plane arrived the six baby objects seemed to enter the main body and the whole thing contracted in size before vanishing.

When Sierra Charlie landed in Labrador at 1.51 a.m. GMT, Howard and Boyd were hustled away for debriefing by USAF and Canadian intelligence officers. Clearly they considered this sighting to be of great significance.

ILLUSIONS OF GRANDEUR

On landing in London later that day Howard and Boyd were summoned to the Air Ministry, but McDonnell was not. When he met Howard in Pakistan some months later during their next flight together he tried to find out what had been said at this meeting, but McDonnell was reminded that this was not a matter for public discussion. Presumably the captain had been reminded of his duty by the Air Ministry.

The media, meanwhile, were informed that the UFO mystery had been solved. It had been an astronomical effect connected with an eclipse – one that had not even started when the sighting took place!

In 1969 the file on the Stratocruiser incident was one of those subjected to the world's first government-funded scientific study of UFOs, when a team of researchers set up by the University of Colorado completed two years' work into the official files of the US government. Physicist Dr Gordon Thayer studied the data, which also revealed that the object seen from the BOAC aircraft was tracked by the radar at Goose Bay, and came up with a proposal.

I'VE NEVER SEEN ANYTHING LIKE IT!

Encounters by aircrew are frequent occurrences, but rarely are they free to talk about them for fear of repercussions from above. Two former colleagues at Dan Air have come together for the first time in seventeen years to relate for *Strange But True?* their own sighting on a flight from London to Malta.

It was 11.34 GMT on 28 August 1978. Captain Lou Cockerill describes the weather as they flew at 33,000 feet over Germany heading towards Frankfurt: 'It was a beautiful day – absolutely clear. Eight-eights blue. As we looked out to the right and at about a 60 degree angle through the aircraft's cockpit roof, we saw this large spherical object.'

It was exceptionally bright white and the size of a bicycle wheel, and it was not alone – as First Officer Paul Coomber confirms: 'I noticed next to it a couple of smaller ones and I pointed this out to the captain sitting next to me. We both looked at it for a few seconds and, as we were watching, they all disappeared in different directions at an incredible acceleration.' This remarkable method of departure is often reported when multiple lights of this kind are witnessed. UFOlogists theorize

Captain Lou Cockerill and crew.

that it may be connected with electromagnetic fields causing the glowing balls of energy to repel one another.

Certainly this vanishing act transfixed Captain Cockerill. He says, 'I spent quite a bit of time in the Air Force firing rockets and things like that, but I have not seen anything accelerate as rapidly as this.' Paul Coomber was equally impressed noting, 'I have never seen anything like it in twenty-five years of flying. It's the only time I have ever seen anything in the air I could not explain.'

Lou Cockerill points out that until that day, he was a sceptic about UFOs, thinking them all to be figments of people's imagination. Now he has changed his mind. 'If I am out at night where there is a nice clear sky, I stare around for some time hoping that I might get another sighting. I have not done so far. However, I do believe there is something out there, definitely.'

He worked out a series of complex mathematical calculations which indicated that the object could have been an optical mirage – a reflection of some other object, possibly the aircraft itself. The image would have been similar to the 'pool of water' effect on the road ahead when driving on a hot, sunny day – the 'pool' is, in fact, a mirage caused by the sky. Both optical rays and radar waves can be bent to create illusions.

Certainly there are aspects of the Goose Bay case that fit this hypothesis well, such as the changing shape and manner of disappearance, and the way the phenomenon 'paced' the aircraft for some minutes close to sunset. That said, Thayer was puzzled by other features. He concluded his analysis with the words: 'this unusual sighting should be assigned to the category of some almost certainly natural phenomenon, which is so rare that it apparently has never been reported before or since'. This seems as close as possible to a government-backed scientist describing an encounter as a genuine UFO – bearing in mind that this term simply defines an unidentified phenomenon, not a spaceship.

Nightmare in the Skies

Mid-air encounters continued unabated until 1978, when a remarkable series of episodes was made public even as they happened. Perhaps the most chilling occurred over the Bass Strait between Australia and Tasmania on 21 October that year. The pilot was twenty-year-old Frederick Valentich, who had little experience of night flying, especially over water, but was otherwise considered competent.

Nobody knows the full story of what happened on that evening as he made a short hop to King Island to collect some crayfish. Nobody knows, because Valentich and his Cessna 182 simply vanished off the face of the earth – but not before the pilot had described a living nightmare in the skies.

Steve Robey was one of the air traffic controllers on duty at Melbourne's air traffic control centre that night. Valentich had filed a flight plan to reach King Island before dark, but just before the intended take-off time he unexpectedly left to have a meal: this delayed his departure and meant he would have to fly the final part over water in the dark. He would also be without radar coverage at his relatively low height once he had passed the Cape Otway lighthouse. Robey says he found it strange that Valentich 'did not request to have the King Island runway lights illuminated'. To do so before take-off 'is the normal way to go', the controller adds.

The Cessna passed the lighthouse at 7 p.m. and from then on Valentich was outside the range of the radar. But about six minutes later his routine reports took a dramatic turn.

'Is there any traffic in my area, below 5000 feet?' he asked Steve Robey.

The controller knew that nothing was supposed to be out there but he checked anyhow, including unscheduled military flights. Nothing else ought to be near the pilot. But something else was in the air according to Frederick Valentich.

Robey recalls: 'He described this other aircraft as being large, possibly a military type with bright white landing lights.'

A minute or two later Valentich reported: 'It's approaching now from due east, towards me... it seems to me that he's playing some sort of game. He's flying over me – two, three times – at speeds I cannot identify.'

Then the young pilot's voice cut in with: 'It's not an aircraft – it's....'

Robey recalls that he was told by the worried young man that the object was 'orbiting over the top of him'. He also described its shape as long and said that it had a 'green light and was sort of metallic-like'.

Now Valentich reported that his Cessna's engine was coughing and 'rough idling'. Finally came the panic-stricken comment; 'Melbourne – that strange aircraft is hovering on top of me again.... It's hovering and it's not an aircraft!'

There followed a period of clicking, with the microphone open but no sounds uttered by the pilot. Then complete silence. Despite launching a search-and-rescue mission as soon as he was overdue at King Island, no trace of the pilot or his aircraft was ever found.

PRESUMED FATAL

The official Australian Department of Aviation accident report published in May 1982 was a masterpiece of uncertainty, terming the location and time of the incident as 'not known', the reason for the accident as 'not determined' and the degree of injury as 'presumed fatal'. This remains the position to this day. The complete absence of any wreckage is another puzzling factor, although there were unconfirmed reports of some debris soon after the crash. The taped recording of the final conversation between Valentich and Steve Robey has never been released.

So what happened to Valentich? Was he abducted by an alien spacecraft? Or did a UFO bring about his death? Both theories are popular with UFO researchers and there are even amazing stories of witnesses who claim to have been told by their alien visitors that Valentich is living with them!

His father, Guido Valentich, still hopes that this may be correct. 'It was a kind of relief regarding my son's involvement with an object buzzing him,' he points out. 'We immediately thought maybe some extra-terrestrial beings had taken him and he probably would be happy. I could not believe that he had ditched in the water and been killed.'

This was a comforting thought, but is it backed by any evidence? Certainly there had been a wave of UFO sightings in the area during the previous week or two, and the media had been full of stories.

The Valentich case is a fascinating detective story which so far nobody has solved. But there are clues. Not only was there his curious behaviour just before take-off, but he is known to have fuelled his aircraft with several times the amount required for such a short trip. Moreover, he took with him a collection of UFO press cuttings, because he was fascinated by the subject.

Guido has little time for the idea that his son may have engineered his own disappearance by inventing a UFO sighting to cover his tracks. 'I could not possibly think about suicide, because my son was very happy with the progress he was making with his flying. He had a girlfriend. He had a life full of activity.' There is also no evidence that Valentich had any criminal associations that might have made an escape to a new life necessary.

But if the short flight to King Island was really all that he intended, why take UFO cuttings with him? 'The main reason,' asserts his father, 'was that he was doing various classes in meteorology and there are certain cloud formations that look like a UFO. But he was no fanatic on this subject. He only became a strong believer that UFOs do exist.'

There is a further suggestion, however, that he may have run across smugglers, who were known to use large nets attached to their aircraft to carry drugs below the waterline. If intercepted by the authorities they could release the nets and there would be no proof of their crime. If another aircraft flew into one of those nets the results could be disastrous. The problem is that suggestions such as this – or, as in another brave theory, that the Cessna was struck by a falling meteorite imply a sudden catastrophe. Yet Valentich spent several minutes on the radio describing what he could see.

What does Steve Robey believe? 'I am convinced that Frederick did not fabricate the story because he sounded so genuine on the radio,' he concludes. 'I am convinced in my own mind that he encountered something strange. Whether it was a UFO or not, I do not know.'

THE KAIKOURA UFOS

Only a few weeks after the Valentich disappearance first hit the headlines, probably the most important aerial encounter of all time took place. This featured all the best aspects of such cases: visual and radar observation made by several different pilots and air traffic controllers. But it added a new dimension – high-definition 16mm colour film which, within hours, much of the world was viewing on TV news bulletins.

The story really began ten days earlier, soon after midnight on 21 December 1978. On duty at Blenheim airbase on New Zealand's South Island, was warrant officer Ian Uffindell, who had twenty-six years' aviation engineering experience and was himself a qualified pilot. He says: 'I was doing my final rounds before retiring for the night, and driving up the tarmac I noticed these lights.' There were three of them, and they resembled aircraft landing lights approaching from the south.

At first Uffindell thought he was watching an inbound aircraft, but the lights did not land and after ten minutes he went to the control tower to investigate. Here contact was established with the radar room at Wellington Airport, just across the Cook Strait.

John Cordy was the senior air traffic controller on duty at Wellington that night. He was very experienced, having worked at busy airports such as London Heathrow. With him was Andrew Herd, and both witnessed the astonishing events which transpired.

ANGELS IN THE NIGHT

Cordy reports: 'We first saw some radar returns off Kaikoura which we joked about, because Valentich had disappeared a couple of months earlier.' Then the call came through from Blenheim about the sighting over the Kaikoura Mountains. The radar echoes were very puzzling. They did not resemble the usual 'angels' – radar-speak for the anomalous propagation effects caused by mirages and temperature inversions. These were 'moving in a random but purposeful fashion... they were making little circuits and going backwards and forwards'.

It was frustrating for Cordy, because the Wellington tower was 70 miles north of the objects with a major mountain range in between so they themselves had no chance of visual contact with the UFOs. Also, virtually no air traffic was scheduled until after dawn. However, ground observers at Blenheim, including Uffindell, noticed that the lights were sending beams down to the ground. He felt they were searching for something. Then they started moving. As this was being reported, Wellington radar captured the targets moving in the same direction.

Uffindell explains what happened next: 'They retraced their steps covering a quarter-circle in the process. I had the distinct impression that what we were seeing was controlled movement and that the large light was like a mother ship controlling two satellites doing its bidding.'

John Cordy was equally baffled. 'We were sure they weren't aircraft, because first they were flying in too tight a pattern and second no aircraft order had been notified to us as to anything being airborne, and they would need clearance from me to operate.'

Meanwhile Captain John Randle, flying a Safe Air Argosy freighter into Christchurch, had spotted some lights off the coast near Kaikoura, 50 miles south of Blenheim. Keith Heine was his first officer on the flight. Wellington radar had told this aircraft to look out for anything near the site of their peculiar radar tracks. Heine says: 'We could see some lights just slightly on our right-hand side and these were moving in what I thought looked to be fairly random movements – but they were just where radar had these returns on their screens.' The lights resembled dull car headlights.

At one point a light was detected on radar, moving at about 120 knots. The crew could see nothing, but Wellington noted that it was heading on a collision course with the Argosy and warned them forcefully of this. However, the light circled around their rear – again unseen by the Randle and Heine.

The Argosy did a quick turnaround at Christchurch and flew back north, deliberately changing course to pass over the Kaikoura region instead of going further west. Another brilliant light was seen and Captain John Randle confirmed he was picking it up on his airborne radar as well.

Eventually a further opportunity was presented when a second Safe Air Argosy was set to leave on its southbound flight to deliver newspapers. Cordy knew that this plane would pass right through the coastal area where the unknown objects were showing on radar screens.

A SKY FULL OF UFOS

By now, Cordy and Herd had tracked an object moving slowly in the south-east which gradually pulled to a halt and stayed there for forty minutes. This was an even bigger mystery for these trained operators, because their radar had a system that ought to have eliminated stationary targets. They checked into the possibility that it was a weather balloon, but this did not prove feasible.

Cordy says: 'We tried everything we could think of, playing with our radar controls to get rid of the target, to see if we could rationalize it. We couldn't.' Andrew Herd's duty was now ended and he signed himself off the roster, but had no intention of going home whilst the sky was full of UFOs.

It was about 3 a.m. when the second Argosy took off, with Captain Vern Powell at the control. Almost immediately he and his co-pilot saw unexpected lights in the sky. 'Out on our left was this large orb hanging in the sky.' It seemed to cause clouds to glow when they passed before it, rather like the moon would do. They confirmed with Wellington that visual and radar targets correlated. This was the clearest proof yet that what was up there was no radar angel. At one point it disappeared and they told Wellington. Cordy confirmed that it had vanished off the radar screen as well, but it soon came back.

The light was visible for fifteen minutes as the Argosy flew over the Kaikoura area. Vern Powell admits that the hairs on his neck stood on end, but Cordy was able to reassure him. 'The radar operator told us it was about 30 miles away, so that was rather encouraging!'

After passing over Kaikoura heading south the Argosy left behind the huge ball of light, which resembled a hovering parachute flare. But they did briefly detect an object streak across their path, looking like a white light and tracked on airborne radar as going at 15,000 kph.

RETURN VISIT

The last radar sighting that night was at 4 a.m. Then all went quiet, until the media picked up the story later that day. Too many people were involved for secrecy, and the air-to-ground radio messages had been intercepted. It became a big story in Australasia.

By chance Quentin Fogarty, TV reporter for Australia's Channel 10, was on holiday in New Zealand at the time. On Boxing Day he received a call suggesting that he should film interviews with the aircrew and prepare a report to bring back home with him. Although cynical at first, he eventually agreed and enlisted the help of a local husband-and-wife camera team, David and Ngaire Crockett.

The interviews with the pilots soon convinced the team that the story had substance. Then Fogarty hit upon an idea. The trip from Wellington to Christchurch and back was a regular delivery run, so he asked Safe Air if they could fly with one of these trips and get some background shots from the flight deck for use with their film. Around midnight on 30-31 December 1978

Fogarty and the Crocketts boarded a Safe Air Argosy piloted by Captain Bill Startup and first officer Bob Guard.

All was very routine at first as they flew south from Wellington, with Fogarty preparing a piece to camera explaining they were passing over the area where it had all happened at about this same time the week before. David Crockett was filming and Ngaire was recording the sound, despite the cramped conditions of the aircraft. The background rumbling noises were horrendous and they were bumped about quite heavily.

Suddenly, the TV crew were told to come to the flight deck. Bill Startup pointed to the lights of Kaikoura coming up below. Yet above this coastal town were some other strange lights in the sky. 'They started as a small pinpoint,' Fogarty explains. 'Then they would grow into this large pulsating glow with tinges of red and orange. They were giving out so much light you could see it either coming on to the cloud or on to the sea. They were bright enough to be lighting up what was below them.'

LET'S HOPE THEY'RE FRIENDLY

David Crockett was not especially impressed by what he saw through the camera lens, as it was difficult to point the camera out of the window and view at the same time, given the angle of the lights below their path. 'To me it just looked like stars or something like that,' he explains. However, from the background excitement it was clear that the aircrew did not know what the lights were, and they were indicating that Wellington radar had these targets on their screens as well.

At first Quentin Fogarty just watched in awe, then remembered his job and began to record some sound commentary. An eerie atmosphere was filling the plane. Ngaire Crockett says she was afraid to touch the side of the fuse-lage as it felt hot. Quentin Fogarty refers to a 'sense of presence' on board. And after landing Captain Startup reported that the plane's outside hull felt slightly magnetized.

At Christchurch the plan was that the film crew should disembark and drive back north the next day, filming interviews with ground observers en route. However, Fogarty now asked if they could fly back to Wellington in the plane and Safe Air agreed. But Ngaire refused to go back into the air after what had happened and her place was taken by Dennis Grant, a local reporter who had turned up after hearing the ground-to-air radio communications.

On the return flight more strange things were seen over the Kaikoura area. All on board were convinced that something was really out there and

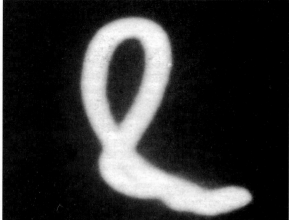

These three images, taken from consecutive frames of the film taken of the major object encountered, show incredible changes of shape in three-tenths of a second. Top: frames N1765, N1766 (the loop) and, below, N1767. The camera was running at approximately ten frames a second. None of the witnesses saw the detail of the loop because it took place so rapidly.

Fogarty recorded on to his commentary the now infamous line: 'Let's hope they're friendly!' His words spoke of a huge white light that appeared as they climbed up through cloud. Crockett attached a 200mm telephoto lens to his camera and saw through it some domed craft. Most of the best shots in his 23,000 frames of film were taken on this return leg, and within the next couple of days, these images were to be seen around the world.

FROM SQUID BOATS TO CABBAGES

The furore created by this sighting was extraordinary. In some respects the 21 December sightings were more important, but the film ensured that the second night seized all the headlines.

However, there were significant problems. Much of the structure that appears in some of the frames is the result of the lens attempting to focus on what were just points of light. There is much debate as to whether the large domed object is also just a product of the focus or had real shape. Bear in mind that shooting shake-free hand-held images with a telephoto lens is difficult enough even on solid ground, let alone inside a rattling cargo aircraft with almost no space to work and only a narrow window to look out from.

Soon afterwards Dr Bruce Maccabee, a US Navy optical physicist and private UFO investigator, flew to New Zealand and Australia to research the case and analyse the film. He believed that one object was as large as a two-storey house and 5 miles from the aircraft, but after much work on a frame in which one light appears to do a remarkable 'loop-the-loop' it was unclear whether this was a real motion on the part of the object or the result of camera shake. This latter view is favoured by most who have studied the case.

Nevertheless, the film undeniably shows some strange lights in the sky, over the mountains and out at sea. So what are they? Most of the conclusions are absurd, from flippant ideas like Santa Claus to seriously offered but still absurd theories such as moonlight reflecting off cabbage patches (impossible because of the radar images and the fact that some of the lights were above the ocean). Astronomical ideas were popular, including meteors and the planets Jupiter and Venus (even though Venus did not rise until after the aircraft landed on its return journey). Perhaps the most reasonable attempt at a solution involved a fleet of Japanese squid fishing boats that used powerful arc lights readily visible from the air. But this fleet was 150 miles off the coast of Kaikoura at the time and so seemed an unlikely source.

WITNESS PERSPECTIVES

Even those best qualified to judge – the witnesses at Kaikoura – have no consensus answer. Ian Uffindell thinks 'it was a controlled craft of some description, and, as there was no logical explanation of it coming from New Zealand or our allies, or anything like that, one can only really assume that it came from out there – that it was extra-terrestrial.' Keith Heine suspects it had a terrestrial origin. 'My own feeling is that it was American technology being tested in some way.' Captain Vern Powell simply prefers to call it 'unidentified' but is furious at the various 'official' explanations, pointing out that he knows what Venus looks like, having flown for thirty-five years, and adding that they saw the distant glow from the squid boat fleet which was well away from where the UFOs had appeared.

Cameraman David Crockett also rejects the rationalist theories, noting that he flew the same route again with Captain Startup a week later. 'I had a 500mm lens with me, infra-red film and everything that I should have had – we saw nothing this time.' This convinces him that the lights filmed on 31 December were genuinely unexplained and not part of the normal environment.

Quentin Fogarty has perhaps the strangest answer of them all. 'It was hard for us to tell whether these were solid objects or just great big saucers of light. I mean, to us they just looked like balls of light. So I never had the feeling of a physical object – a spacecraft as some people call it. I did not get the feeling that there were entities on board controlling me. I felt that whatever they were was all self-contained and that they were like some hypnotic bright light with a sort of spiritual quality.'

John Cordy insists 'the radar was not playing up'. As to the idea of atmospheric mirages or angels being to blame, he agrees that 'the possibility is there' but 'these images stayed on the radar for so long in the same positions that it made them unlikely to be angels'. He further adds that the official theory – that the UFO was Venus – is ridiculous. 'The pilots could have seen a planet – maybe. But I'm damned sure my radar would not have shown Venus. If it did, we could have sold it to the Americans for a fortune. They've been trying to map the planets with radar for years! I have never seen a planet on my radar screen in the whole of my thirty-four-year career.'

UFOlogists have proposed their own idea: that the lights may be natural atmospheric energies created by geological forces in the Kaikoura mountain range. Similar light phenomena – known to researchers as UAP or earthlights – have been encountered above mountains across the world from the Pennines in England to the Hessdalen valley in Scandinavia. Laboratory experiments have even duplicated and filmed these energies, which glow by way of incandescent gases or plasmas.

Which – if any – of these answers applies to the Kaikoura case may never be known.

KEEPING THINGS UNDER WRAPS

The Kaikoura case is an exception. According to Graham Sheppard, a former British Airways pilot and now working for another major airline, aircrew are notoriously reluctant to report their UFO sightings.

One of his two personal encounters from the air occurred aboard a British Airways aircraft bound from Scotland to London in 1967. Passing over northern England under control of Preston radar, his captain was advised that unidentified traffic was heading towards the plane. Moments later all three flight deck crew – including Sheppard – saw a disc-like object streak beneath them at fantastic speed. Sheppard described it as about 30 feet in diameter, with a raised central portion and estimated that it was doing a speed of 1000 mph. Neither his captain nor Preston radar decided to file an official report on the matter. In the next thirty years of flying he came upon this reluctance many more times and has kept a log of accounts from other civilian pilots who have seen things but were unable to make official reports.

I have experienced the same attitude with airlines, who seem to fear that it may jeopardize passenger confidence if it emerges that their planes regularly encounter UFOs. This is difficult to justify, as there have been so many sightings that virtually no major airline in the world is uninvolved. One day in July 1981, for example, I received a call from a ground crew member at Liverpool Airport. He insisted on anonymity, saying he would be sacked if it was known that he was reporting this incident to me. At 2 a.m. that day the crew of a Dan Air cargo flight had seen a white light over the Point of Ayr on the Dee estuary. Investigation later revealed an eye witness on the Wirral peninsula who had seen both the UFO and the aircraft from ground level. However, no official report was filed by the airline.

Between April and July 1991 half a dozen mid-air encounters took place in the skies over southern England, two of which were recorded on radar (one at Heathrow and one at Gatwick), several of which were subjected to CAA (Civil Aviation Authority) investigations, but all of which failed to find a solution. In one case Gatwick radar even vectored another aircraft out of the way of the UFO as it left, heading out over the Sussex coast. Airlines involved included Alitalia, British Airways, Britannia and Dan Air.

In most of these cases the object was described as a small, dark lozenge shape. Speculation that it is a form of toy balloon designed to look like a UFO and which can reach surprising altitudes has been examined by UFOlogists, with inconclusive results. However, there is no doubt that something has been occurring and on at least one occasion the CAA considered the risk of collision to be significant.

Clearly civilian life is at risk and the public surely have a right to know about such matters. Fortunately, the former secrecy has been replaced by a spirit of cooperation in Air Staff 2A, the Ministry of Defence now responsible.

In February 1991 there were brief reports in the Manchester press that a strange light had been seen by an aircraft landing at the airport there. I sought the MoD's help to investigate and was amazed to receive news of impressive ground witnesses – four air traffic controllers who had been on duty in the control tower. They had chosen to say nothing in public, but had submitted their story to the MoD according to official guidelines.

I was eventually able to talk with one of these witnesses, who had thirty-five years' experience as a radar controller. He confirmed that they had all seen what the crew of a Manx Airlines plane had witnessed as they landed after a flight from the Isle of Man at 7.19 p.m. on 21 February. The UFO was a brilliant band of coloured light that rushed across the sky and baffled all those concerned. But despite considerable investigation, no clear-cut solution was found.

Sightings still continue. Perhaps the most recent involved a jumbo jet passing over the Derbyshire Peak District in January 1995 on its way to Manchester airport. The crew ducked when a triangular object flew straight at their cockpit and then rushed past their wings. One possibility is that it was a bright meteor. The true extent of the evidence from aircrews may well never be known, but it clearly runs into hundreds or even thousands of sightings.

SOURCES

FURTHER READING

The following codes will help to identify the major topics covered by the books in this list: G(Ghost), H(Healing), M(Miracles), N(Near death experiences), P(Poltergeists), R(Past Lives), T(Time anomalies), U(UFOs). Books marked with an asterisk are generally sceptical in tone.

Baker, Robert, *Hidden Memories,* Prometheus, 1992 (R*)

Bardens, Dennis, *Psychic Animals,* Robert Hale, 1988 (G,H)

Blackmore, Susan, *Dying to Live,* HarperCollins, 1993 (N*)

Coleman, Michael (Ed), *The Ghosts of Trianon,* Aquarian, 1989 (T)

Condon, Edward (Ed), *Scientific Study of UFOs,* Bantam, 1969 (U*)

Devereux, Paul, *The Earthlights Revelation,* Blandford, 1990 (U)

Epstein, Gerald, *Healing Visualisations,* Bantam, 1994 (H)

Fogarty, Quentin, *Let's Hope They're Friendly,* Angus & Robertson, 1984 (U)

Forman, Joan, *The Mask of Time,* Macdonald & Jane, 1978 (T)

Gauld, Alan & Cornell, T, *Poltergeists,* Routledge Kegan Paul, 1984 (P)

Goss, Michael, *The Evidence for Phantom Hitchhikers,* Thorsons, 1984 (G*)

Green, Celia & McCreery, C, *Apparitions,* Hamilton, 1975 (G)

Harris, Melvin, *Sorry, You've Been Duped!* Weidenfeld & Nicolson, 1986 (*)

Hodgkinson, Liz, *Spiritual Healing,* Piatkus, 1992 (H)

Hynek, J Allen, *The UFO Experience,* Corgi, 1974 (U)

Keeton, Joe & Moss, P, *Encounters with the Past,* Sidgwick & Jackson, 1978 (R)

Klass, Philip, *UFOs: The Public Deceived,* Prometheus, 1983 (U*)

Lorimer, David, *Survival?,* Routledge Kegan Paul, 1985 (N)

Manning, Matthew, *The Link,* Corgi, 1973 (G,P)

McKenzie, Andrew, *The Seen and the Unseen,* Weidenfeld & Nicolson, 1987 (G)

McClure, Kevin, *The Evidence for Visions of the Virgin,* Thorsons, 1984 (M)

Morse, Melvin & Perry, P, *Transformed by the Light,* Piatkus, 1992 (N)

Nickell, Joe & Fischer, J, *Secrets of the Supernatural,* Prometheus, 1988 (G,H,N,R,U*)

Playfair, Guy Lyon, *This House is Haunted,* Souvenir, 1980 (P)

Randles, Jenny & Hough, P, *The Afterlife,* Piatkus, 1993 (G,N,P,R)

Randles, Jenny & Hough, P, *The Complete Book of UFOs,* Piatkus, 1994 (U)

Randles, Jenny, *Time Travel,* Blandford, 1994 (T)

Randles, Jenny & Hough, P, *Encyclopedia of the Unexplained,* O'Mara, 1995 (G,M,N,R,T,U)

Schull, Bill, *The Psychic Frontiers of Medicine*, Ballantine, 1977 (H)
Spencer, John & Ann, *Encyclopedia of Ghosts and Spirits*, Headline, 1993 (G,P)
Startup, Bill & Guard, B, *The Kaikoura UFOs*, Hodder & Stoughton, 1981 (U)
Steiger, Brad, *Project Blue Book*, Bantam, 1977 (U)
Wilson, Colin, *Poltergeist!* NEL, 1981 (P)
Wilson, Ian, *Mind Out of Time*, Gollancz, 1981 (R*)

USEFUL ADDRESSES

The following organisations and magazines will provide more information on the paranormal. The same codes apply. If no letter is shown they cover most, or all, of the topics in this book:

Absent Healing Centre (H), Roland Thomas House, Shrewsbury Hospital, South Shrewsbury, SY3 8XF
Afrinews (G,U), PO Box MP49, Mount Pleasant, Harare, Zimbabwe
The Anomalist, PO Box 12434, San Antonio, TX 78212, USA
ASSAP, 64C Boxley Road, Maidstone, Kent, ME14 2TW
Aura Z (G,H,M,P,U), PO Box 224, Moscow 117463, Russia
Australian UFO (U), PO Box 1894, Adelaide, South Australia 5001, Australia
BUFORA's UFO Call (U), Premium rate information line of latest news (UK only) 0891 – 121886
Dead of Night (G,P), 156 Bolton Road East, New Ferry, Wirral, Merseyside L62 4RY
Enigmas (G,P,U), 41 The Braes, Tulibody, Clackmannanshire, Scotland FK10 2TT
Fate Monthly, PO Box 1940, 170 Future Way, Marion, OH 43305, USA
Fortean Times, PO Box 2409, London, NW5 4NP
International UFO Reporter (U), 2457 West Peterson Ave, Chicago, IL 60659, USA
New UFOlogist (U), 71 Knight Avenue, Canterbury, Kent, CT2 8PY
Nexus (H,M), PO Box 30, Mapleton, Queensland 4560, Australia
Omega Project (N), Dept of Psychology, University of Connecticut, Storrs, CT 06269, USA
Psychic News (G,H,P), 2 Tavistock Chambers, Bloomsbury Way, London WC1A 2SE
Quest (U), PO Box 2, Grassington, Skipton, North Yorkshire BD23 5UY
Reincarnation International (R), PO Box 26, London WC2H 9LP
Skeptical Inquirer (*), PO Box 229, Buffalo, NY 14215, USA
Society for Psychical Research/Psi Researcher (G,N,P,T), 49 Marloes Road, London W8 6LA
Spiritualist Association (G,H,P), 33 Belgrave Square, London SW1X 8QB
Spiritualist National Union (H), Stansted Hall, Stansted, Essex
Strange Magazine, PO Box 2246, Rockville, MD 20847, USA
The Skeptic (*), PO Box 475, Manchester M60 2TH

The author would be pleased to hear from anyone who wishes to report their strange experiences. A stamped addressed envelope will help facilitate a reply. Write c/o 11 Pike Court, Fleetwood, Lancashire FY7 8QF.

ABOUT THE AUTHOR

Jenny Randles has researched strange phenomena all over the world and is the author of more than 30 books describing her work. She has a diploma in media communications and has often used her specialist expertise to good effect with media productions.

In 1975 she wrote a TV feature on UFOs, researched and presented a six-part series of documentaries about the supernatural for radio some years later, and is currently making a film about the work of an UFOlogist with the BBC. For several years she was a 'paranormal agony aunt' for the ITV teletext service, answering viewers' questions on their problem page.

She became associated with *Strange But True?* when the pilot programme was developed in 1993 and now serves as story consultant to this top-rated series.

Jenny has lectured on the paranormal in places as diverse as a casino on the Australian Gold Coast and in the British Houses of Parliament, where she briefed politicians at their request. Her articles have featured in a wide variety of newspapers from the *Guardian* to *Weekly News,* and have appeared in magazines such as *She, Bella,* and *Celebrity* as well as in specialist journals across the board from the *New Scientist* to *Police Review.*

A life member of BUFORA (British UFO Research Association) and with NARO (the Northern Anomalies Research Organization) for the past 22 years, Jenny is also British representative for America's J Allen Hynek Center for UFO Studies – one of the world's most respected scientific organizations. She is a founder member of ASSAP (the Association for the Scientific Study of Anomalous Phenomena) and is also a member of the Society for Psychical Research.

Amongst the many areas that she has investigated first hand are alien abductions, coincidences, past-life memories, spontaneous human combustion, time-slips and UFOs.

Jenny is co-author with Peter Hough of *Strange But True?, The Afterlife* and *The Complete Book of UFOs* (all published by Piatkus). She is currently working on her new book entitled *The Paranormal Sourcebook* as well as a secret project involving near death experiences!

Jenny lives on the Fylde coast of north-west England.